DATE DUE

JUN 2 0 1998	
FEB 2 0 2003	

| UPI 261-2505 | PRINTED IN U.S.A. |

MARION H. BIRD

MATHEMATICS FOR YOUNG CHILDREN

An active thinking approach

ROUTLEDGE

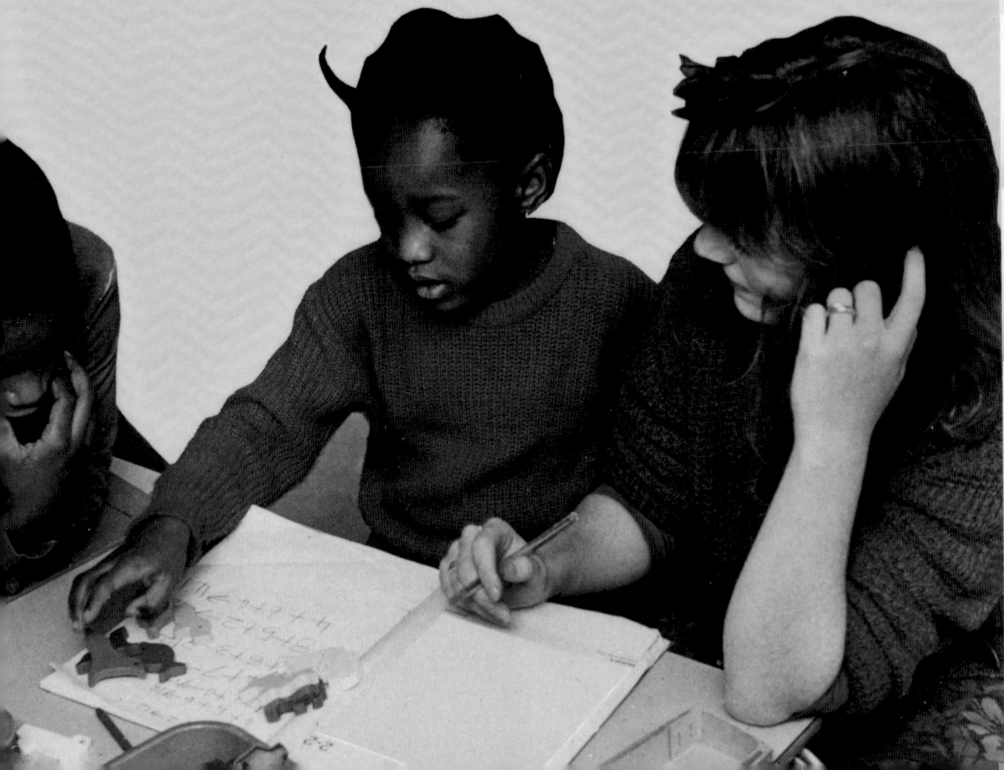

MATHEMATICS FOR YOUNG CHILDREN

In recent years, increasing stress has been placed on the importance of giving the under-sevens a good start in mathematics. This book shows how children as young as four and five and of all abilities can be encouraged to carry out their own mathematical explorations whilst covering the content of a prescribed curriculum.

A substantial part of the book is taken up with actual case-studies of children working with Marion Bird in a reception classroom, fully illustrated with examples of the children's work. These case-studies are then analysed to show how a prescribed syllabus can be effectively covered through an investigational approach: a point which is of paramount importance to teachers concerned with the introduction of the National Curriculum. The role of the teacher, too, is examined carefully in order to identify those parts of a teacher's repertoire which seems to be particularly fruitful in encouraging young children's active mathematical thinking. Throughout, readers are encouraged to apply and amend ideas to suit their own particular circumstances.

Marion H. Bird is a Senior Lecturer in Mathematics Education at the West Sussex Institute of Higher Education.

MATHEMATICS FOR YOUNG CHILDREN

An active thinking approach

Marion H. Bird

London and New York

First published 1991 by Routledge
11 New Fetter Lane, London EC4P 4EE

Simultaneously published in the USA and Canada
by Routledge
a division of Routledge, Chapman and Hall, Inc.
29 West 35th Street, New York, NY 10001

© 1991 Marion H. Bird

Typeset in Palatino by Leaper & Gard Ltd, Bristol
Printed and bound in Great Britain by
Biddles Ltd, Guildford and King's Lynn

British Library Cataloguing in Publication Data

Bird, Marion
  Mathematics for young children : an active thinking approach.
  1. Great Britain. Primary schools. Curriculum subjects: Mathematics.
  Teaching
  I. Title
  372.70440941

ISBN 0-415-06479-1. – ISBN 0-415-05951-8 (pbk)

Library of Congress Cataloging-in-Publication Data

Bird, Marion H., 1955–
  Mathematics for young children : an active thinking approach /
  Marion H. Bird.
     p.   cm.
  Includes bibliographical references (p.   ) and index.
  ISBN 0-415-06479-1. – ISBN 0-415-05951-8 (pbk)
  1. Mathematics–Study and teaching (Elementary)   I. Title.
QA135.5.B533   1991   90-23425
372.7–dc20   CIP

CONTENTS

LIST OF FIGURES

Sometimes a single unnamed child will be referred to as 'she' and sometimes as 'he'. This is to avoid clumsy expressions such as 'he/she' or 'his/her'.

PREFACE
AND ACKNOWLEDGEMENTS

Recognition of the importance of children learning mathematics in an active fashion has increased rapidly since the publication of the Cockcroft Report in 1982. Indeed, the DES document 'Mathematics from 5 to 16' (1985) goes as far as to claim that the aim of teaching mathematics should be to show it 'as a process, as a creative activity in which pupils can be fully involved, and not as an imposed body of knowledge immune to any change or development' (p. 4). To date, however, little has been written about how such an aim might be fulfilled with the younger age-groups of children in school. This book is intended to help fill the gap by focusing on how 4 and 5 year olds can be encouraged to work actively at mathematics.

It is not my intention that the book will give direct recipes for action of the tips-for-teachers sort. What I hope, however, is that it will influence readers' actions through contributing to a development in thinking. I hope it will serve to intensify some perceptions and challenge others whilst all the time increasing sensitivity to possibilities in the classroom. It is meant very much as a working document, open to individuals to apply critically to their own situations. I hope this lack of finality is implicit throughout the whole book, but I have also attempted to make it explicit in various ways, for example through the inclusion in the chapters in part III of questions/ suggestions aimed directly at the reader. These questions are not intended to be viewed as exercises seeking straightforward answers, but to indicate some of the many possible starting-points for further work. They represent points where I am sure more could be said.

The main readers I have in mind are teachers on in-service mathematics courses; teacher-researchers, teacher-educators, education researchers and students in the later stages of their training. Anyone concerned with young children, however, might find points of interest.

Many people helped make my original study and this resulting book possible. They are too numerous to list altogether, but I particularly want to mention my gratitude to the following: Eira Gill and Betty Jackson who, as headteacher and reception class teacher in the school in which I worked, showed considerable enthusiasm, co-operation, patience and thoughtfulness; Brenda Briggs for the hours of thought-provoking discussions and challenging questions throughout the time I was engaged in the study; John Mitchell for his painstaking reading of the draft of each chapter and his fruitful suggestions and, above all, for his insights and inspiration over many years which have contributed in no small way to my own perceptions of learning and teaching mathematics; and finally to all the children on whom this book is based.

Part I
SETTING THE SCENE

1

SOME QUESTIONS

There is growing evidence to demonstrate that top infants, juniors and secondary school pupils can work at mathematics in an active way, carrying out their own explorations. Let us examine an example of such an approach to mathematics:

Context I involved a class of 11 and 12 year olds in trying to find numbers which have an odd number of factors. Having deduced that all square numbers would have an odd number of factors, different pupils had different ideas as to what could be explored next. One of the ideas was to choose a particular odd number and try to find rules for producing numbers with that number of factors.

Consider the extract from Anne's write-up of her exploration into generating numbers with exactly three factors (figure 1.1).[1]
    An analysis of Anne's account suggests that she has been involved, even at this stage, in at least the following processes: seeking an efficient method; comparing; searching for relationships; abstracting; recognising equivalences; recognising differences; making conjectures; generalising; structuring; being systematic; ordering; calculating; recording; reasoning; explaining. These processes, and others (see figure 1.2), seem to be typical features of working actively at mathematics.

But what about younger children? Can children as young as 4 and 5 become engaged in such processes in mathematics?

Consider the following snippets from observations of children in their first two days in a reception class:

The teacher is reading the class a story and showing them the pictures. She holds up a picture of a teddybear.
Anne-Marie (4.10): He's in the bathroom.
            Teacher: Why?
    Anne-Marie: Because he's holding a towel.

3

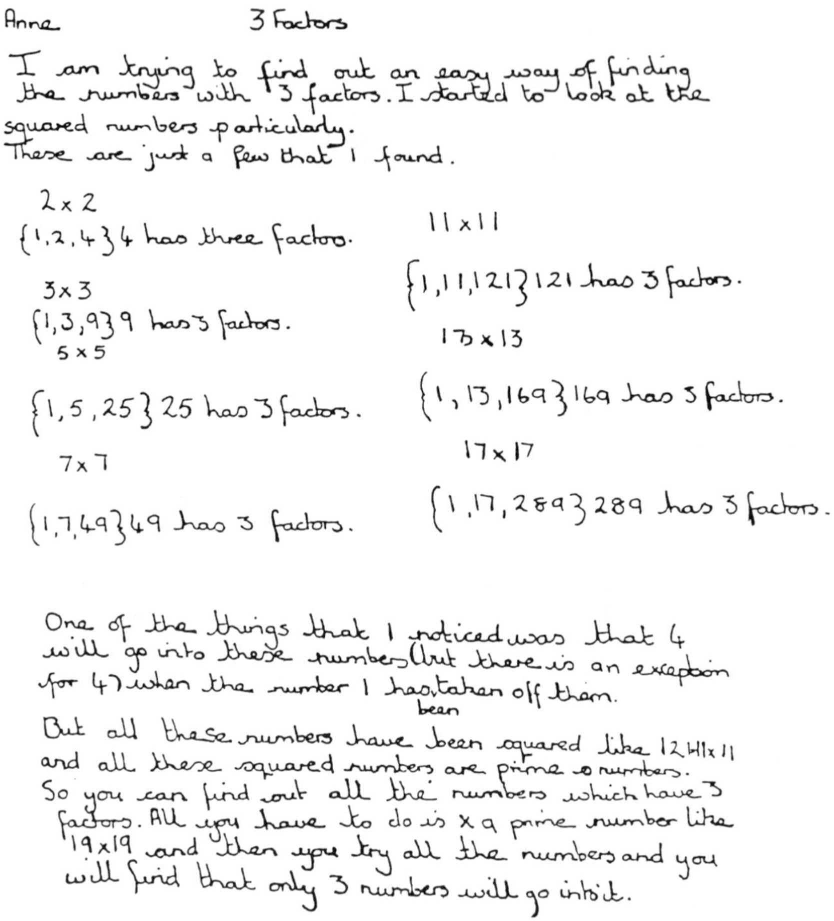

Anne   3 Factors

I am trying to find out an easy way of finding
the numbers with 3 factors. I started to look at the
squared numbers particularly.
These are just a few that I found.

2 x 2
{1,2,4} 4 has three factors.

11 x 11
{1,11,121} 121 has 3 factors.

3 x 3
{1,3,9} 9 has 3 factors.

5 x 5
{1,5,25} 25 has 3 factors.

13 x 13
{1,13,169} 169 has 3 factors.

7 x 7
{1,7,49} 49 has 3 factors.

17 x 17
{1,17,289} 289 has 3 factors.

One of the things that I noticed was that 4
will go into these numbers (but there is an exception
for 4) when the number 1 has taken off them.
                  been
But all these numbers have been squared like 12 H1x11
and all these squared numbers are prime numbers.
So you can find out all the numbers which have 3
factors. All you have to do is x a prime number like
19 x 19 and then you try all the numbers and you
will find that only 3 numbers will go into it.

Figure 1.1 Anne's exploration into generating numbers with three factors

The children had each been given their own name cards. Luke (4.08)
picks up Jemma's (4.11) and says, 'Her name's not the same as mine.'

Luke is playing with some plastic animal shapes. Taking the ducks
from the pile and putting them to one side of his table he remarks, 'All
the ducks, right, can go in the water.'

Steven (4.09) is tidying up the meccano. Suddenly he exclaims, 'Somebody's put those in here' and starts removing some bolts from the big
box containing the rest of the apparatus and putting them in the
empty plastic container where they really belong.

Matthew (5.00) is playing with a toy lorry whose back lifts up but
Steven has one which does not. Looking at Matthew's lorry Steven

4

Figure 1.2 Some processes which are characteristic features of working actively with mathematics

asks him, 'Can I play with that one?' Matthew replies, 'No, but you can play with that one', pointing to a further lorry a short distance away. This lorry's back also lifts up but the toy is a different colour from Matthew's. Steven hesitates. Matthew adds, 'They're both the same aren't they?'

The teacher is showing the children a book in which flaps lift up to reveal things underneath. The children keep guessing what will be under the flaps.

Vanessa (4.11): Helen and I have done tracing before. We went to playschool together.

Helen (4.08): It's like this at playschool.

MB: How is it like this?

Vanessa: There's the same chairs and the same tables, but there's not these. (*pulling out a tray slotted under her table*)

Steven is playing with Clive (4.09). Steven says, 'There's a fire. I'll go and get some water.' He goes across the other side of the room to the lorries which he had been playing with earlier. Picking two up he says, 'I call them water lorries.'

Everyone is sitting on the mat. Noticing one of the children has just stood up, Ilona (4.11) remarks, 'I think that little boy wants to go to the toilet.'

Ben is looking through a book of pictures, and decides that a very stylised picture is 'clouds'.

Matthew remarks, 'Every night at 5 o'clock I keep getting toothache.'

When asked what he is doing with some plasticine John (4.11) says he is 'making all sorts of cakes' and goes on to point out which are cherry cakes (red balls of plasticine on top of yellow plasticine) and which are toffee cakes (brown plasticine).

Here we see young children involved in such processes as reasoning, explaining, making connections, seeing differences, seeing equivalences, classifying, sorting, including, excluding, generalising, making conjectures, representing, defining and interpreting. These were some of the processes listed in figure 2.2 but here they are occurring in non-mathematical contexts. Numerous other snippets could have been included. Indeed, to engage in such processes seems to be an essential and all-pervasive part of human activity.

If it is 'natural' for young children to engage in such processes, should it not be possible for these to play a more significant role in the children's mathematics too?

This is a tiny glimpse of some reception children in the 'home corner' of the classroom on their second day at an infant school:

Helen (4.08) and Vanessa (4.11) come into the 'house'.

Vanessa: I'll tidy the place out. (*To Helen*) You're out.
Helen: What do you mean, 'I'm out'?
Vanessa: You're out. I'll tidy the place out. (*Both girls 'tidy up' the house, putting things in sensible places, for example a saucepan on the stove, a baby doll's dress in the cot.*)
Helen: I'll be Mummy.
Vanessa: No, I'll be Mummy.
Helen: You can be Mummy in a minute. You can be Mummy another day. All right Vanessa? ... Vanessa? (*Vanessa is continuing to tidy without looking up. Helen continues to tidy for a little while too. Then both girls leave the house. After a few minutes, Lisa (4.05) comes in, followed by Helen again. Then Emmaline (4.11) knocks on the door and Helen opens it.*)
Helen: Do you want to come in before I shut the door? (*Emmaline is looking round at something else in the classroom.*)
Emmaline: I've got these sweets. (*She is carrying a bag of sweets from the classroom 'shop'.*)
Helen: I'm Mummy. Be quiet everyone! You can make a cup of tea. (*To Emmaline.*) How many cups?
Emmaline: One for you, one for her and one for me. (*pointing to Helen, Lisa and herself in turn*)
Helen: And you better make one for the other one (*meaning*

6

Vanessa?). Oh! She might not be able to come now might she? (*Emmaline puts out three cups and saucers.*)

Emmaline: (*To Helen*) Do you take sugar or tea?

Helen: Teabags.

Emmaline: This is the tea-cosy isn't it? (*picking up a piece of material which earlier she had used as a duster and earlier still as a cloth to wipe the baby doll's bottom!*) Where's the sink? (*picking up the toy kettle from a cupboard*) Do you know where the sink is, please?

Helen: Come here. Give us the kettle. I'll put some water in it. (*Helen pretends that there is a tap in the wall over a table and pretends to fill the kettle. Emmaline takes the saucepans off the stove and puts them away in the cupboard. Helen puts the kettle on the stove.*)

Helen: Have you made a cup of tea?

Emmaline: Not yet. I'm just putting the teabags in (*pretending to put something in each of the three cups*). (*Anne-Marie (4.10) and Vanessa knock at the door. Emmaline opens it.*)

Emmaline: Could you two go up to the shop and get two of them biscuits for me please? (*Anne-Marie and Vanessa go to the classroom shop and come back with two 'biscuits'. Emmaline picks up the bag of 'sweets' she had fetched earlier and starts to pass these round, now as 'biscuits'. She takes the two others from Anne-Marie.*)

Emmaline: Thank you. Here you are. You can have those to eat. (*Ben (4.09) comes in.*)

Emmaline: Is there another cup? See if there's another cup in there.

As well as providing further evidence that children engage in a variety of processes (which processes feature naturally in the above?), this extract reveals reception children sustaining an activity by themselves, continually developing the situation and controlling it.

But how often do we allow 4 and 5 year olds the freedom to take initiatives within activities which we set up under the label of 'mathematics'?

The lights in the corridor flickered. Matthew (5.00) says, 'I just saw the lights go on and off. Why do they do that?

(*Steven (4.09) notices two little pieces of sellotape stuck to the door frame of the home corner.*)

Steven: What's this here?

MB: I expect something was stuck up with it.

Steven: What?

7

Ilona (4.11) is working with some plasticine on a table with two girls who have already been at the school a term. She asks them each in turn, 'What are you called?' Then, referring to some pictures on the wall she asks them each, 'Which one did you make?'

Lisa (4.05) is sitting with some other children round a table. She asks them, 'Who was sitting here first?'

(*Luke (4.08) has been drawing a picture.*)
Steven: What's that?
Luke: Father Christmas.
Steven: What's that mauve then?

Emmaline (4.11) sits on a large beanbag in the classroom for the first time. She feels the little polystyrene balls inside it, through the material, and asks, 'What's in here?'

The above are just a few of the numerous questions I witnessed children asking during their first two days at school.

The natural curiosity of young children is, of course, very marked. This shows itself not only in their questioning but also in the extent to which they are absorbed in exploring unknown situations. To cite just one of many examples, several of the above children spent time on their first day at school investigating what was in the containers in the class 'shop'.

Can we devise mathematical situations which continue to allow young children's curiosity to come to the fore?

When they came in from playtime during their first morning at school, Ben (4.11) and Lisa (4.05) were told that they could play with the unifix cubes which were on their table. Both started to make sticks of unifix which grew taller and taller (they were holding the sticks vertically).

Ben: I'm going to put mine right up to the ceiling.
Lisa: Mine's going up to my bedroom.
Ben: Mine's going to be higher than that. Mine's going to be higher than the stars.

Then Ben's tower of cubes toppled. He looked dismayed but laid down what was left in one piece in his hand so that it was flat on the table. He moved the stick up to the shorter edge of the table and put more and more cubes on it until he reached the other end of the table. He had to stand up to complete it and move round to the other side of the table. Having completed the stick he took out some more unifix from the box and started to build a second stick, this time along the longer edge of the table with one end touching the end of the completed stick.

Ben: I'm going to do this right up to the end of the table.

This he did. As he was adding more cubes he kept checking that the new stick was not knocking the other stick off the table: if the first stick moved a little he would put it back in place. He made various comments as he was carrying out his self-imposed task such as 'It's nearly there', and asking 'How many of these do you think I'll need?'

Given the freedom to do so, young children frequently set themselves challenges, often quite daunting ones at that.

When we involve young children in activities under the label 'mathematics', how often do we give them space to set their own challenges?

Helen (4.08) is playing with some plastic shapes. She sorts out eight black squares from the rest and sets them out in a straight line. Then she starts to put green squares on top of the black squares, one on each. With two still required, she runs out of green squares and comments, 'I don't have enough!' Then she finds a further green one and says 'Now I need one more.' Whilst hunting for more green squares she finds a green *triangle*. She looks surprised, laughs and exclaims, 'What's this? A triangle!'

Anne Marie (4.10) has a tin of plastic animals in front of her. She takes out two orange ducks, two pink cats, two red kangaroos, and two blue ducks, putting them in their pairs underneath one another. Emmaline (4.11), who is sitting at the same table, remarks, 'You've got two orange ducks and two blue ducks, haven't you?'

John (4.11) and Ben (4.09) are sharing a pot of beads and a piece of string. Ben remarks, 'I'll do the same amount as you. All right?' and takes a turn at threading. Having threaded four beads Ben asks, 'Have I done the same amount?' John contemplates the string for a while then replies, 'Do two more.' Ben decides differently, however, and says, 'I'll do three more', adding, 'I'll pass you then!' Ben threads on three more beads. John says, 'I'll do two more then' to which Ben continues, 'When you've done these two more, I want to do some. All right John?' to which John replies, 'No, I want to do a little more, I'll just do five!' Ben questions, 'Five?' John adds three more beads to the string and says, 'Two more' (meaning two more left to go?), adds another one and says, 'There we are.' Ben, sounding impatient comments, 'You've done *four!'* John says, 'I said five' and starts to pick up another bead. Ben says, 'I'll do the last one ... the hard one ... all right?' John nods and lets Ben put the final bead onto the string.

In these short extracts (recorded during the children's first two days at school) we see these young children structuring their activities in ways which involve them in various aspects of mathematics. Of their own

9

volition, the children have been engaged in items which feature on the mathematics syllabus for the reception class in their particular school (determining the number of elements in sets; comparing sets; recognising shapes etc.). Some of these items were also in evidence in the 'home corner' extract (pp. 6–7). It is also interesting to note the ocurrence of some of the processes discussed on p. 3 and p. 6 in the above episodes.

How can we make use of children's own potential for creating mathematics when we are planning tasks?

Some of the items in which the children have been involved spontaneously are ones which would not have featured until the children's second or third term when following the school's planned scheme of work for the reception class. It is all too easy to make misguided assumptions as to what children will be able to do or not do; what they will need to practise; what they must do before they can cope with something else, etc.

How often do we overlook children's actual capabilities when they arrive at school? How can we become more aware of these?

Reception class children are often set tasks such as those in figure 1.3.

Where is the potential for making conjectures, generalising, defining, deciding on rules, etc.?

Where is the scope for children's own questions, initiatives, control, etc.?

How can we be certain that the tasks will not be too easy? Or too difficult?

Where is the scope for intellectual challenge?

The number syllabus for a reception class looks something like this:

Cardinal number: Finding the number of
elements in sets.
For a given number, finding
an appropriate set.

Ordinal number: Using and recognising 'first',
'second', 'third', etc.
Using knowledge of the
ordering of numbers.

Learning number names.

Writing and recognising numerals.

Comparing numbers of objects; recognising and setting up relationships; more, less, same.

Figure 1.3 Typical reception class tasks

Simple addition.

Simple groupings.

Recognising and finding 'half' of objects.

All these possibilities are based on the numbers 0 to 10.

How can we cover a syllabus and yet, at the same time, involve children in carrying out their own mathematical thinking?

11

2

SOME BACKGROUND DETAILS

For the last two years I have been working with 4 and 5 year old children in a reception class, concentrating on the issues implicit in the questions raised in chapter 1.

The school takes children as 'rising 5s', that is, in the term in which they will be five. This means that the youngest children with whom I worked were 4 years 8 months old. The children who start in school in January or April stay in the reception class for two terms but those who start in September are there for three terms. This means that the oldest children with whom I worked were 5 years and 10 months.

The catchment area is urban with council flats and owner-occupied small terraced houses predominating. The school building is an old Victorian one, opened in 1900. The classroom used by the reception children is typical for its age: tall windows set high in the wall (hence the children cannot see out easily), painted brickwork, no central heating, etc. The room is completely enclosed, small and cramped. As such it is very unlike some of its modern counterparts, with no carpeted corner or access to practical areas, etc. There is, however, a small sink in one corner and the class teacher has also succeeded in squeezing in a 'home corner' and a small 'shop'.

Whilst I was working with the class, the number of children varied from seventeen one term to thirty-seven another term. The tables were arranged to accommodate groups of between four and eight children, but when there were thirty-seven in the class there was not room for everyone to sit down at once!

The class teacher usually organised mathematics so that different groups were doing different activities at the same time. She would either talk to the children altogether at the start of a session, detailing the different tasks with everyone listening, or she would ask all the children to continue with some previous activity or to start some simple task, then she would go round the room talking with the groups separately, thus setting up a staggered start. To avoid disruption as much as possible I wanted to arrange my teaching to fit within this overall organisation, hence much of the work reported on here has been carried out by small groups of children.

Having worked with the class for a few sessions, I found that I was amassing so much material that it was becoming overwhelming and could never be reported on in its entirety, other than superficially. Hence it seemed sensible to restrict the inquiry somehow. To this end, I made the following decisions:

1   I would focus on 'number' as a specific area of mathematics, rather than looking at all possible parts of the subject. I chose this area not because I felt that work on shape, measures, etc. was unimportant, but because it was number which seemed to be the major concern of the infant teachers I was meeting on courses.

2   For each of my sessions with the children I would concentrate my subsequent analyses on just one group of them, to be decided in advance of the start of the activities. For at least four terms I would try to analyse the work of as many groups as possible, so that I could encompass the whole gamut of abilities, attitudes, personalities, etc. (whatever we might mean by those words). Then for two terms I would concentrate on the *same* group each session so that I could address myself to issues such as how children's engagement in the activities seemed to develop over a period of time.

3   I would concentrate on analysing sessions whose beginnings I had specifically planned. Much mathematics came about through the children's spontaneous activities in the home corner (as on pp. 6–7), or in the class shop, but for the purpose of this study I would ignore those. This was far from decrying such valuable experiences, but simply to study something about which little had previously been written.

4   I decided not to investigate the exciting possibilities of using micro-computers with young children. There are so many issues to be explored in relation to this that would necessitate lengthy studies in themselves.

The class teacher worked to a syllabus for number. This is the one which can be seen on pp. 10–11. I was concerned to respect the fact that this syllabus was in operation in the school and intended to see how (if?) it could still be covered through my activities with the children.

I visited the school one day a week, each Monday. I spent part of the day working with the children myself and the rest of it observing the children's reactions to work set by the class teacher. It seemed important to have opportunities to observe so that I could make some attempt at slotting some of the activities I initiated with the children into their general classroom life. This included their participation in activities not specifically labelled 'mathematics': I watched them writing up their 'news', painting, playing, going to assembly, etc. Also, from Tuesdays to Fridays the class teacher kept for me any written records of the mathematics carried out by the group of children on whom I was focusing on Mondays.

I often put a tape recorder on the table of the group currently being studied. Several video tape recordings were also made.

After each session with the children, I tried to draw out and focus on my perceptions of what had happened as soon as possible. In particular I concentrated on forming impressions of the nature of the mathematics which arose; the initiatives shown by the children; and features of my role which might have facilitated or inhibited the children working actively at mathematics. I used the audio and video tape recordings to help with the analyses. As the time progressed, some of my thinking altered: some earlier ideas were challenged; some previously hidden assumptions were brought out into the open; and various points were viewed from different angles. Through their own analyses of the data I had collected, other people also contributed to my evolving thinking (see p. 122).

Trying to communicate all the wealth of data collected would be an impossibility, as would trying to convey all of the analysis. It could also easily become very tedious to read. After much deliberation, I have decided to present accounts of six sessions only (see chapters 3 to 8), but I will describe them in some detail. Obviously this has necessitated making a choice and some readers may wish to know my reasons for including the particular case-studies I have. These centred on the following factors:

1   I wanted to include sessions with different groups of children so that readers could gain an impression of the activities of a wide variety of individuals. On the other hand, I wanted the same group to feature in two of the sessions (see chapters 3 and 7) so that readers could compare them.

2   Obviously the class teacher formed various impressions of the mathematical abilities of the children in her class. I wanted the episodes to be reported on here to involve children who spanned these apparent abilities. Readers may be particularly interested to know that the children involved in the activities described in chapter 6 were ones whose mathematics gave the teacher most cause for concern.

3   I wanted to choose sessions which would provide a wide variety of points for the subsequent analyses.

4   I wanted to avoid the temptation of only including the 'best'. I have worries about aspects of the case-study described in chapter 7 in particular.

5   So far I have implied that I view the case-studies and the subsequent analyses as somehow distinct. I am well aware, however, that in the very act of describing an episode, I am bringing my own perceptual framework into play: it would be misleading to think of the case-studies as raw data. Within the limits of a book, the nearest I can get to providing raw data is to give a transcript of a tape recording of part of a session on which readers can base their own interpretations (see chapter 8).

The analyses in chapters 9, 10 and 11 centre mainly on the six case-studies, but mention is made to a few other sessions where particularly appropriate examples were provided.

I could have ordered the book differently. I could have started with the issues I wished to raise about the mathematics, the children's initiatives and my role, using items from my work with the children as illustrations, instead of grouping all the case-studies together. I decided, however, that readers might want to see the context of any such illustrations and giving details of whole episodes shows how activities developed. Moreover, the structure I have chosen allows the reader to work at different levels: an overall and uncluttered impression of the sessions can thereby be gained before delving into any separate analyses.

Further introductory remarks to the analyses can be found on pages 83 and 149.

Part II
CASE-STUDIES

3

CIRCLE ARRANGEMENTS

ORGANISATION

This was an activity with a group of four children: Ilona (5.04), Matthew (5.05), Sam (5.03) and Jemma (5.04). The rest of the class were also working in small groups on a variety of different ideas. I was circulating round the groups. A tape recorder was left on the table where Ilona, Matthew, Sam and Jemma were.

ACTIVITY

I gave out a sheet, like the one shown in figure 3.1, to each child and asked, 'What can you say about what you've got?'

Matthew said, 'There's three circles down, three circles up and three circles in the middle.' Jemma said, 'There's a big square outside and a little square inside', to which I asked, 'Which is the square outside?' Jemma pointed to the rectangle bordering the design and replied, 'I meant this big hexagon there!' I asked the group if it were a hexagon. Jemma immediately changed her mind back to it being a square! Matthew, however, said it was a rectangle. I asked him what made him think that. He explained, 'A square is that big ... a little bit shorter', marking off an appropriate amount of one of the nine smaller rectangles. Sam joined in by saying, 'I think it's a rectangle with ten circles in each one.' This switched the focus of the conversation. Jemma counted the circles and made it nine. Matthew also counted and said it was Sam who was wrong. Sam re-counted and made it nine circles this time. I asked, 'What do you think happened when you made it ten?' Sam quickly replied, 'One more.'

Matthew then announced, 'I know something. We can count them altogether!' I asked him what he meant. He started to point to each of the circles in turn saying, 'Count that one and that one ...' and seemed set to continue like this for each one! I asked him if he would like to do that, then, to which he said, 'Yes', and started counting quietly.

I thought I would try to encourage Ilona to say something. I asked her

19

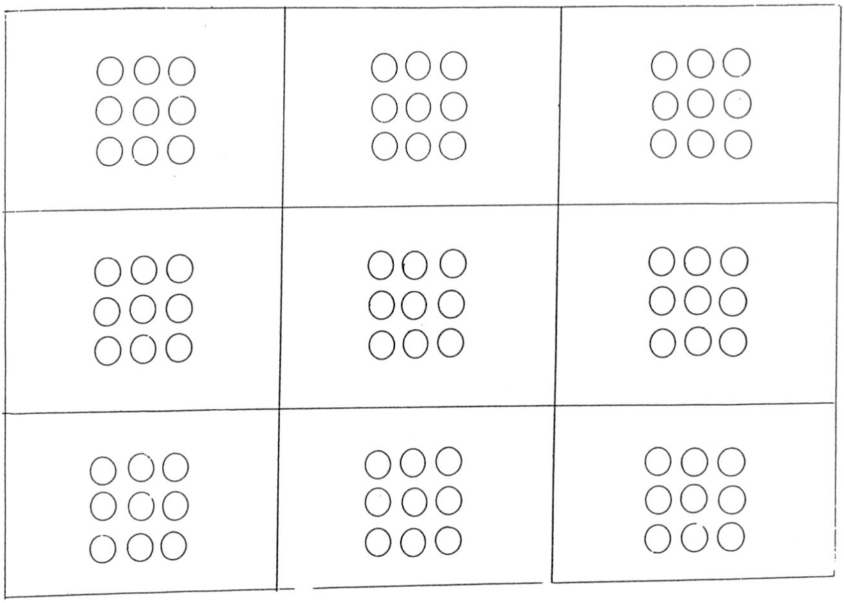

O O O O O O O O O
O O O O O O O O O
O O O O O O O O O

O O O O O O O O O
O O O O O O O O O
O O O O O O O O O

O O O O O O O O O
O O O O O O O O O
O O O O O O O O O

Figure 3.1 The basic sheet for the 'circle arrangements' activity

what she could say about the sheet. She said, 'There's a line of circles there, a line of circles there and a line of circles there', pointing in turn to the three rows of circle arrangements across the page. Jemma added, 'They're all round.' Meanwhile Sam had been counting quietly, along with Matthew, and he announced, 'All these together make fifty-one.' (It was interesting that he had ended up with the correct number of units: perhaps he would be able to arrive at the actual total, eighty-one, if he were helped with the names for some of the multiples of ten?) Jemma started to count as well, but loudly. Matthew objected, saying, 'There's too much noise, I can't do mine!' I agreed that it was difficult to count when people were talking and Jemma said in that case she would not count now. Matthew started again, this time loudly himself. He continued confidently and competently up to forty-nine. He hesitated after this but Sam interposed, 'Fifty.' Matthew carried on, 'Fifty-one, fifty-two . . .' until fifty-nine after which Sam interposed, 'Sixty.' (It was interesting to note that, contrary to my earlier thinking, Sam's knowledge of the names for the multiples of ten seemed very secure indeed.) Matthew was off again until after he had reached sixty-nine whereupon he paused but this time himself added, with emphasis, 'Sixty!' I pointed out that we had just had sixty and it would be strange if we had it again. Sam said, 'Seventy.' Matthew kept going until after seventy-nine whereupon he said, 'And the next one is . . .' to which Sam added, 'Eighty.' With apparent glee Matthew finished with, '*Eighty-one!*' I commented on it being such a big number. Matthew then announced, 'I know how to write eighty-one', and added, 'it's not a one and an eight', to which Sam continued, 'eight and one.' Both Sam and Matthew pencilled '81' on their sheets but Jemma also wanted to write the number and wrote '18'. Sam said that this was eighteen and continued, 'Eight and one, one and eight.' I asked, 'So it makes a difference which way round you put the numbers then, does it, Sam?' to which he replied that it did. Noticing that Ilona was looking confused, I added that I knew that the children had not been considering numbers as large as that in class previously and that some of them might be wondering what we were talking about, but we had found out a little about them and could return to them another day.

I then showed the children the sheet as in figure 3.2 and invited them to 'Have a look at what I've done.' They commented about some of the circles being coloured in. Sam said, 'You've coloured three on each one.' I asked Ilona if she thought that was right. She counted two of the sets of three circles and said, 'Yes.' I said, 'I've coloured three spots on each as you said. I'd like you to choose a number and colour that number of spots on each one.' Matthew started shading in circles on his sheet straight away! I asked him which number he had chosen: he had chosen eight. Then Ilona chose six, Sam five and Jemma four. I watched whilst the children started, observed that they seemed to know what to do and left them so that I could see other groups.

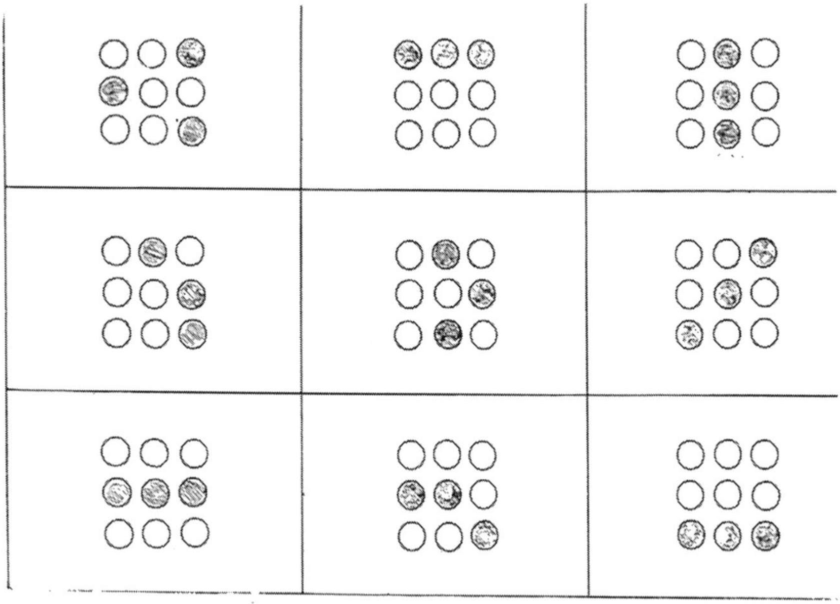

Figure 3.2 My sheet

21

Jemma was the first to finish her sheet. As can be seen from figure 3.3, she made just two different arrangements of four spots, her first two rows being of one sort and the bottom row of another sort. At one point she called across to me to say that she had shaded six spots in by mistake. I asked what we could do about that. Matthew said, 'I know: rub some out!' and Ilona suggested, 'Cross two out.' Jemma fetched the class rubber and erased two spots, then re-counted to make sure that she was indeed left with four. She wanted to keep the rubber because she said, 'I might get a six again!' I agreed that she might colour in six but added that someone else might need the rubber so I would put it back on my way to see the next group of children. The tape recorder picked up that at one point later she shaded in *five* spots in one of the rectangles and worked out that she needed to rub out one spot, which she did.

When Jemma finished her sheet, I suggested that she might work with Ilona. The tape recorder picked up that Ilona was very definite about how her sheet should be completed. For example, she said to Jemma, 'Do a different pattern ... not like that ... go down', and later, 'Now do the same pattern as you've done there.' At one point Jemma suggested, 'I know: if you do two, I do three, you do three and I do two and I do the next one it would be fair wouldn't it?' Eventually, however, Ilona decided that she wanted to carry on on her own and her completed square can be seen in figure 3.4.

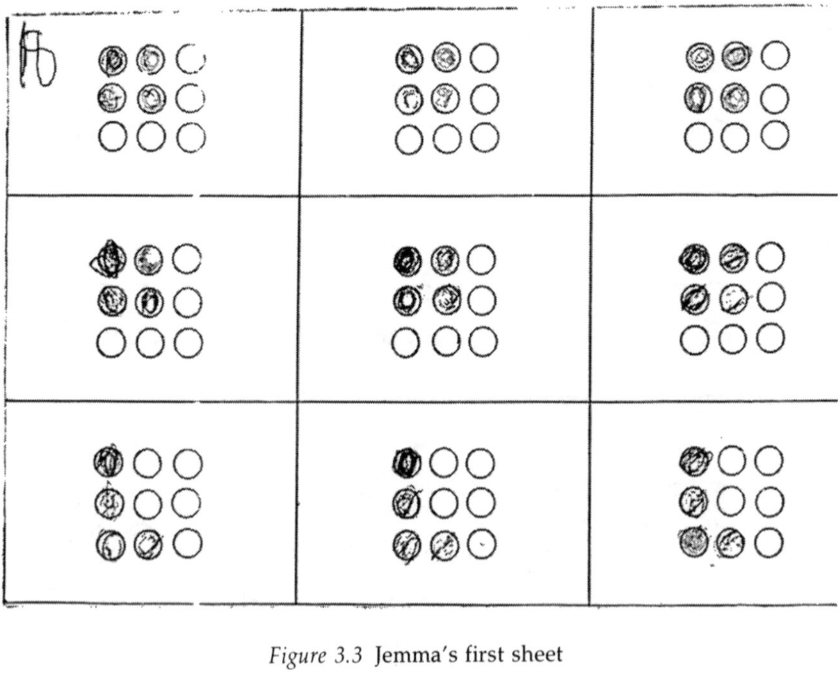

Figure 3.3 Jemma's first sheet

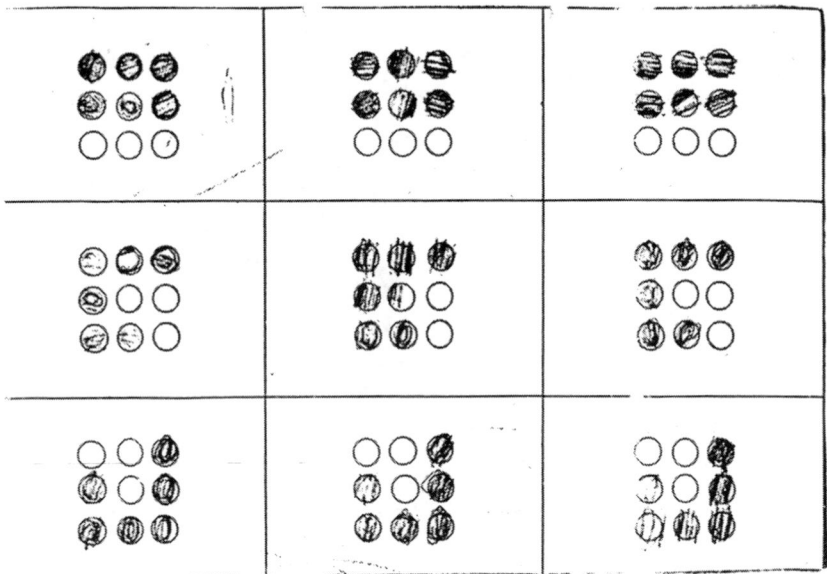

Figure 3.4 Ilona's sheet

Jemma wanted to do sets of two spots on another sheet. Part way through her task she told me, 'If you put them next to each other there, it's all right', pointing to the two shaded spots in one of her rectangles which looked like that in figure 3.5, 'but if you put them next to each other at the top, it's not', pointing to the circles in a blank set (figure 3.6).

She went on to show some other shadings which she would allow, each of which had the two spots arranged side by side. Her completed sheet (figure 3.7) indicates that she kept to that self-imposed rule.

Sam's first sheet can be seen in figure 3.8. It is interesting to note how he has utilised the pattern highlighted in figure 3.9 in eight of the rectangles. He moved this basic design around in different orientations with no repetitions. When I asked him, 'What can you tell me about yours?' he went from pattern to pattern in the order shown in figure 3.10, saying, 'That one's different from that one', each time. I picked out two of his patterns which were not adjacent in the order he had imposed on them (see figure 3.11) and asked, 'What about that one and that one?' to which he replied, 'That one's facing that way and that one's facing that way!' pointing to the single shaded spot on each. Indicating the two illustrated in figure 3.12 I asked again, 'What about that one and that one?' He explained, 'That one's facing up and that one's facing down!'

For a second sheet Sam chose *one* for his number of spots to be shaded,

23

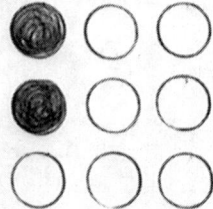

Figure 3.5 Jemma's set of two spots

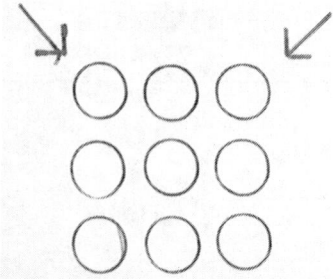

Figure 3.6 Jemma felt that colouring these two spots would not be 'all right'

announcing this with some humour! He hurtled through this, producing the very systematically executed sheet shown in figure 3.13. Going through his sheet, in reading order this time, he said that he had, 'One in the first one, one in the second one, one in the last one; one in the first one, one in the middle one, one in the last one; one in the first one, one in the second one . . .', and I joined in with him, 'one in the *third* one.'

Matthew also decided that each of his eight-spot arrangements would be different. On one occasion when I went over to the group he pointed to the blank spots in his completed configurations and said for each one, 'That goes there', revealing that his attention was now focused on the different positions of *one* spot. Having completed seven arrangements he commented 'I haven't got another space on ones.' (Actually, two of his seven arrangements were the same but I decided not to comment on that, wondering if he would notice it himself.)

I suggested that Sam might bring his one-spot sheet and come and work by the side of Matthew (they had been sitting diagonally opposite one another). Looking at Sam's sheet Matthew said, 'He's only done one colouring in and he's left all the rest out.' I agreed with him and asked what he, Matthew, had done. He said, 'I've left one out.' Matthew then explained his problem to Sam: 'I haven't got another space to leave like that in another circle.' Both the boys concentrated hard on Matthew's paper, trying to find some different arrangements. They used Sam's one-spot paper to help,

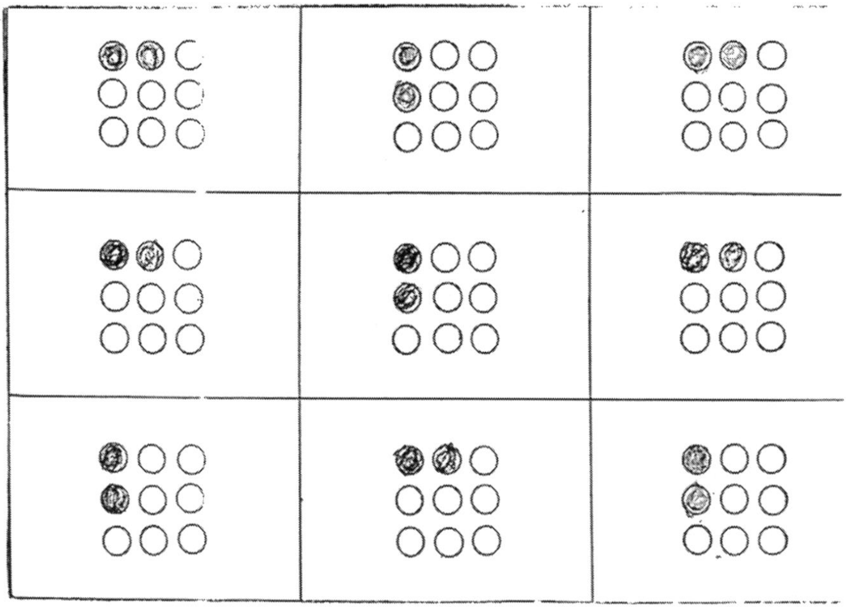

Figure 3.7 Jemma's second complete sheet, showing her two-spot pattern

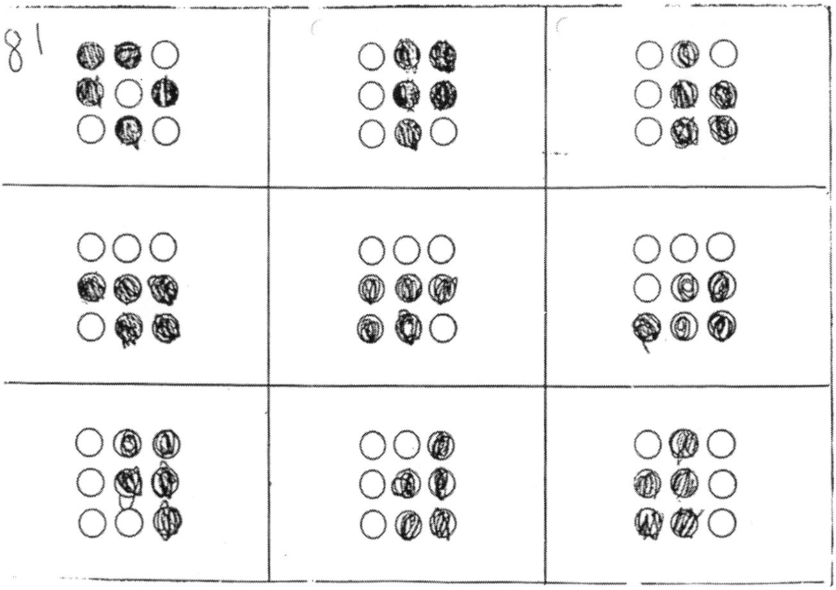

Figure 3.8 Sam's sheet

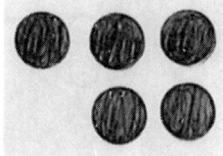

Figure 3.9 Sam's basic pattern

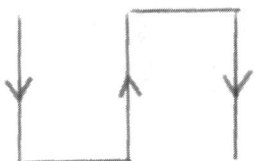

Figure 3.10 The order of Sam's pattern

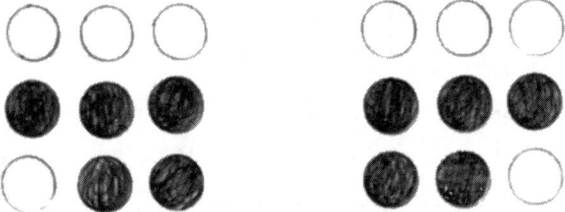

Figure 3.11 Two patterns not adjacent in the order Sam imposed on them

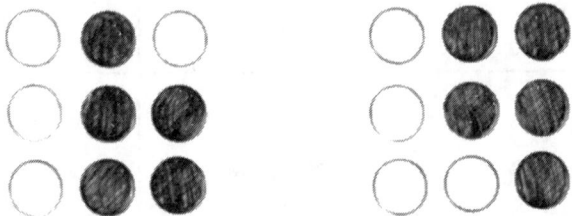

Figure 3.12 Sam's pattern facing up and down

checking Matthew's arrangements against Sam's to see what was left. This enabled them to come up with two more examples (see figure 3.14 for the completed sheet). Sam was able to express the connection between his and Matthew's work. He commented, 'He hasn't coloured in one but I have coloured in mine and he's coloured in all the rest and I haven't coloured in all the rest.' I asked if he could tell everyone else what he had noticed. Pointing to the appropriate sheets he explained, 'There's eight white ones

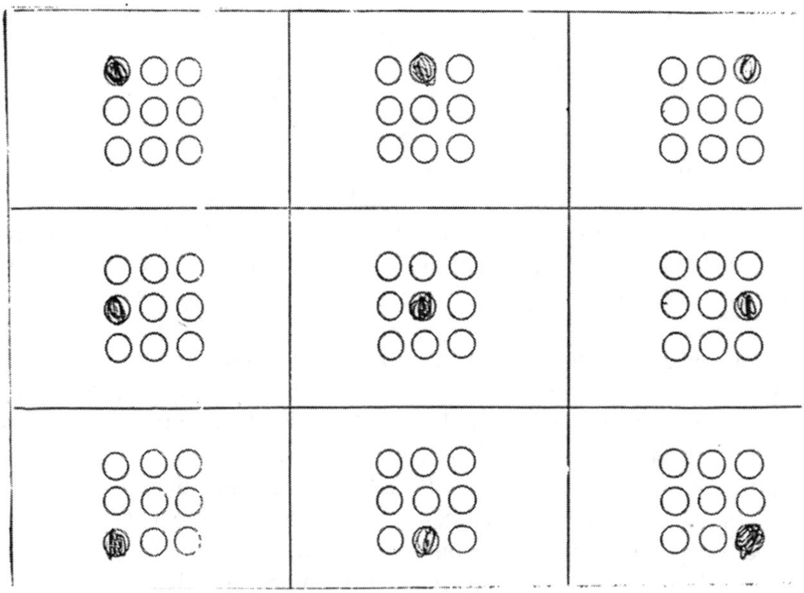

Figure 3.13 Sam's second sheet, showing his pattern of single spots

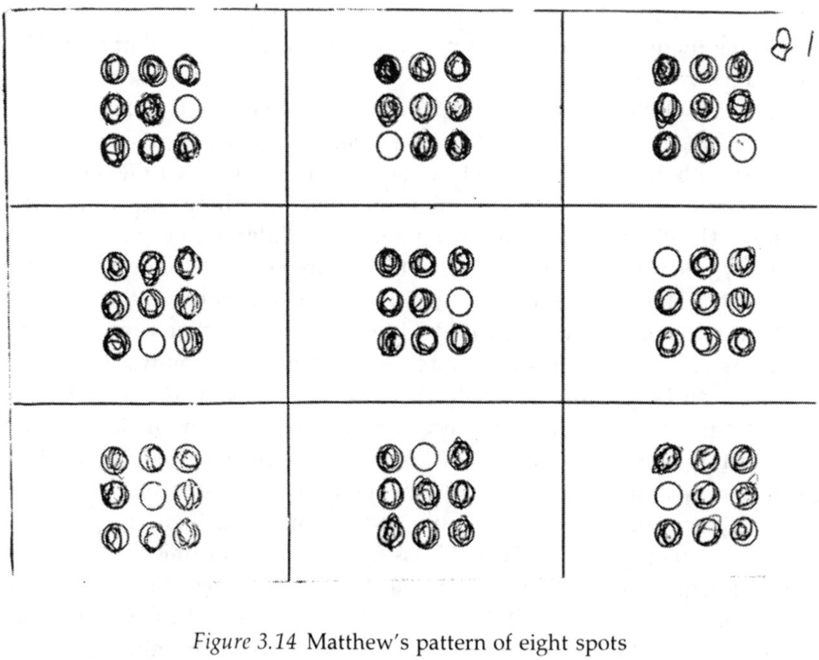

Figure 3.14 Matthew's pattern of eight spots

27

there and there's eight grey ones there and there's one grey there and one white there.' I continued, 'So where you've done grey, Matthew's done . . .', to which they both added 'White' and I continued, 'Where you've done white, Matthew's done . . .', to which they both added 'Grey'. I commented about the patterns being 'sort of the opposites of each other.'

Throughout the session the children made all sorts of spontaneous comments other than the ones I have included in the accounts of individuals above. For example, towards the beginning of the episode the tape recorder picked up Matthew saying, 'Eight and eight and eight', and then (because Sam was shading in five spots?) commenting 'I've got more than you: six, seven, eight.'

I photocopied the children's sheets to keep a record of them and started my next session with the group by inviting them to cut them up along the straight lines (to form nine rectangles). I also asked them to think what they could do with the pieces. I left them whilst they were cutting.

Matthew's idea for what to do with them was to 'Glue them on a piece of paper.' I commented 'We've just cut them up!' Jemma, however, extended the idea by saying, 'Yeah . . . we could glue them on a piece of paper though . . . put them where you *want* to put them; go and put them next to one another perhaps.' This met with approval from the rest of the group. Later, once they had finished their cutting, Matthew announced, 'I've got a good idea! We could make the classroom pretty!' When I asked how, he continued, 'We could glue them on the classroom wall!' I said that we *could* but that I thought the class teacher might not be very pleased, so perhaps we could glue them on to a piece of paper as they had suggested at first! They seemed happy about this.

I gave the children a sheet of paper each and some glue to share. They set about sticking on their pieces. When they had completed their sheets, which they did without any supervision, I asked them each to tell me something about their own design and to think if there was anything they could write about it. (The class teacher was encouraging the children to begin to write. If necessary, she would write down what the children wanted to say, so that they could copy it. I did the same, to fit in with what was familiar to the children.)

Photo-reductions of two of the children's sheets, together with what they wrote, are shown in figures 3.15 and 3.16. A lot of discussion was centred on these, as can be glimpsed from further comments about just one of them, Jemma's (figure 3.15). The tape recorder picked up Jemma making several spontaneous comments about what she was doing such as, 'I had twos going across and twos down' (at the point when some of the group's separate pieces became muddled up), and 'If you count them altogether . . . ten . . . it makes . . . *nine*'. When I asked her what she might say on her paper, though, she said 'I writed about it' [sic]. I pointed out that she had not actually done that yet. A little later she said 'Nine'. I asked 'There are nine what?' to which she replied 'Dots'. I asked 'Are there nine dots?' She

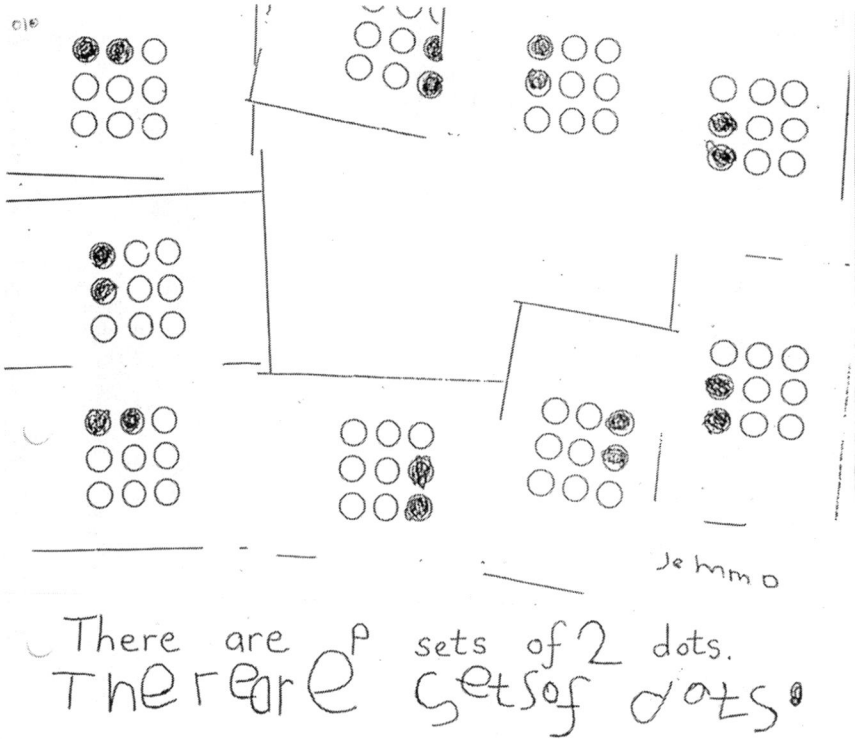

There are p sets of 2 dots.

Therare setsof dots.

Figure 3.15 Jemma's sheet and comments

thought, and said 'Nine *sets* of dots I think' I asked if she wanted that written and she said that she did. I wrote 'There are . . .' whereupon Jemma exclaimed, 'I'll put the number there!' and put in 'p' meaning '9'. I continued '. . . sets of . . .' and again she stopped me and said 'I can put the number two in', which she did. As can be seen from figure 3.16, when she copied the sentence she left out the 'p' and the '2' as she had already written them!

On a later occasion I put the children's sheets out again so that they could all see what each other had done and try to read what was written. Looking at her own sheet, and with some help from the others and from me, Jemma read slowly, 'There are "p" sets of two dots.' I asked if that made sense. Jemma said 'No it doesn't', but did not offer a correct alternative. The others looked again at what was written. Suddenly, Ilona exclaimed 'That's a *number*!', referring to the 'p'. I asked which number it was. Matthew said 'That's number nine' and re-read 'There are nine sets of two dots.' I asked, 'So there are nine sets of two dots. Does that make sense?' Ilona said, 'Two dots', as if confirming that that was all right. I asked, 'Are there nine sets?' Matthew said, 'I think there might be!' Ilona counted the sets of dots and

Figure 3.16 Sam's sheet and comments

confirmed that there were nine, but Jemma counted the blank dots in one of the rectangles, thus arriving at seven. I asked, 'Is Jemma counting what Ilona was counting?' Ilona was emphatic that she was not and recounted the *sets* of dots, showing Jemma what she was doing. Jemma then claimed 'They keep on counting those two', pointing to two sets on the paper (meaning that the others had counted these two sets twice?). Then she recounted the sets herself and found that it *was* nine. Sam claimed that the 'p' was the wrong way round and re-wrote it correctly. Jemma then wanted to write this herself and did so. I commented that perhaps that was why she had read it as 'p' to start with, because it was the wrong way round.

4

SIX BY SIX SQUARES

ORGANISATION

This was an activity with a group of six children: Lisa (5.00), Lianne (5.03), Alan (4.11), Adam (5.03), Hayley (4.10) and Jody-Blue (5.01). It started originally as a ten minute activity, given to the group after they had finished something else and whilst I was collecting in work just before lunch. Details about how it continued are given within the text below. A tape recorder was left on the table where the group were sitting.

ACTIVITY

I gave each of the children a piece of squared paper as in figure 4.1, and put some red, yellow and green colouring pencils on the table where the group were sitting. Lianne had already remarked that it was time for lunch! I suggested that whilst they were waiting they could 'have one of these little pieces each and colour it in using the coloured pencils.'

I left the children. The tape recorder revealed that they did not talk about what they were doing whilst they were carrying it out but chatted about other things (for example 'Your brother is called P. Clarke isn't he?' 'Yes, Peter Clarke!').

When I returned to the group I was surprised to see the amount of structuring that several of the children had put into their colouring. I asked individuals to tell me about what they had done. I invited them to colour in further squares of paper when they had finished their first ones. Lianne was not very enthusiastic about that (but did so) whilst others were very keen, for example Adam, who said 'I'm going to do lots and lots and lots and lots and lots and lots of them!'

This is what the children did in the ten minutes, together with some of their comments:

Lisa

Lisa was the first to finish her first square (see figure 4.2). When asked, 'What

32

Figure 4.1 The basic squared paper

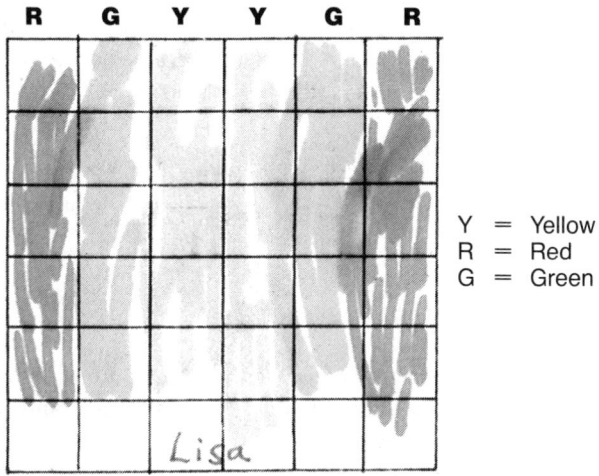

Figure 4.2 Lisa's first square

can you tell me about what you've done?' she replied 'I've done a set of red, a set of green and a set of yellow; and a set of yellow, a set of green and a set of red', in a definite rhythm so that it fell into two phrases.

She then completed figure 4.3. This was the only example of someone apparently paying little attention to the squares. When asked what she could say about it she pointed out the colours, referring to them in a set of three (green, yellow, red) and a set of four (yellow, red, green, yellow), again the groupings being suggested by the rhythm in her voice, but this time not reflecting any obvious pattern.

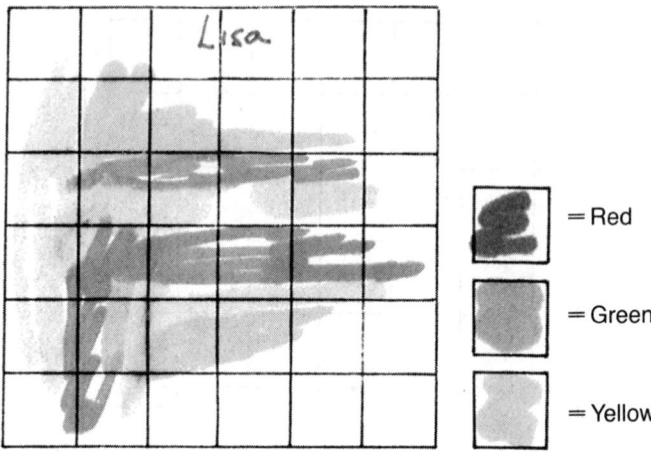

Figure 4.3 Lisa's second square

She went on to complete three more squares hurriedly and said at the end that she had 'done lots'. I did not have a chance to ask her about these last three, although there would have been plenty to discuss.

Hayley

Hayley completed figure 4.4 first. She said 'I've done green, yellow, red;

green, yellow, red'

in this sort of rhythm:

as if grouping the green, yellow, red together and recognising the repetition. I commented 'You've got a pattern, haven't you?' and added 'Would you like to colour another one?'

Hayley then quickly completed the square in figure 4.5 and remarked that she had 'Two red, two yellow, two green.' I said, 'You've done one red, one yellow, one green; two red, two yellow, two green' (actually now reading off the colours in her first example in the reverse order to which she had read them, but I was not aware of this at the time).

I asked, 'What might you do next?' Hayley replied 'Green . . .' then, as if changing what she had been going to say, 'Three yellow, three red.' I asked, 'Do you think that will fill your piece of paper?' to which she responded, 'I don't know.' Later she showed me the square in figure 4.6. She had used green because the other children were using the red pencils. With apparent satisfaction she said, 'I've done it. It just fits!'

She then went on to complete the square shown in figure 4.7. I asked

34

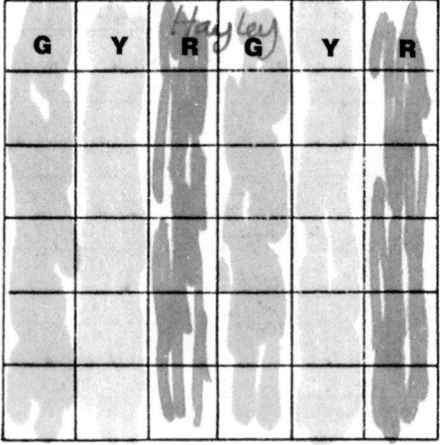

Figure 4.4 Hayley's first square

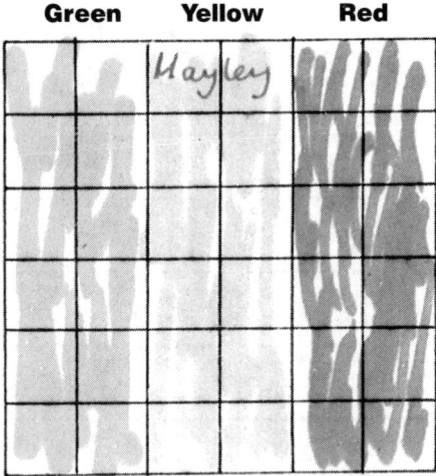

Figure 4.5 Hayley's second square

'Isn't that the same as what you did before?' She said, 'No, that was red, yellow, green. This is yellow, red, green!'

Alan

Alan coloured in the two squares shown in figure 4.8. As can be seen, he decided to keep some squares 'empty.' Having finished the first one he said, 'I've got a pattern', and proceeded to call out the colours of the squares from left to right across the paper, line by line, as though he were reading a book. I could not discern any particular structuring in the way he said the colours.

GREEN   **YELLOW**

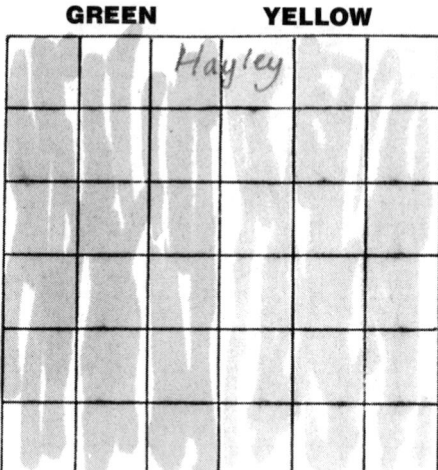

Figure 4.6 Hayley's third square

Y   R   G   Y   R   G

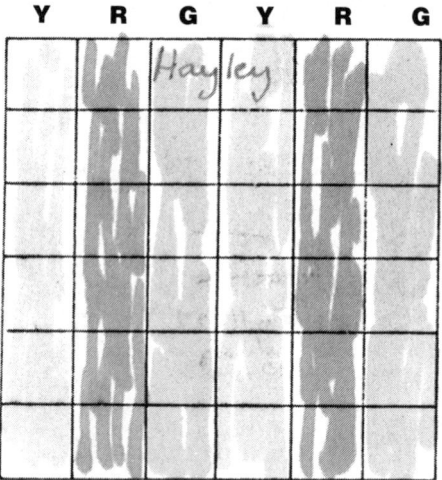

Figure 4.7 Hayley's fourth square

Adam

Figure 4.9 shows what Adam completed in the time. He worked very carefully, colouring in each square individually. I did not have a chance to talk with him about his square.

Jody-Blue

Like Lisa and Hayley, Jody-Blue coloured in stripes for her first example, in the following order: yellow, red, green, yellow, red, green. She then broke

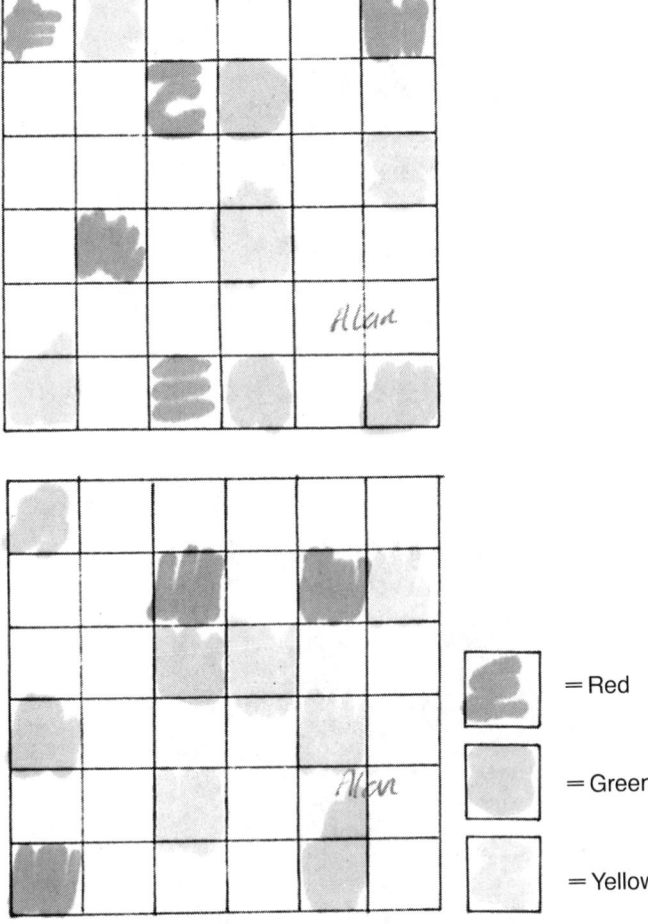

Figure 4.8 Alan's two squares

away from this idea entirely and completed the square shown in figure 4.10. Later she commented that she had 'made triangles' and that she had coloured in 'halfs'.

Lianne

Lianne's first example is shown in figure 4.11. When asked what she could say about it she said, 'A set of reds, a set of yellows and a set of greens.' I asked where the set of yellows was and she pointed out the three patches of yellow. I asked, 'So how many sets of yellow have you got?' to which she replied, 'Three', I asked similar questions about green and red. She said

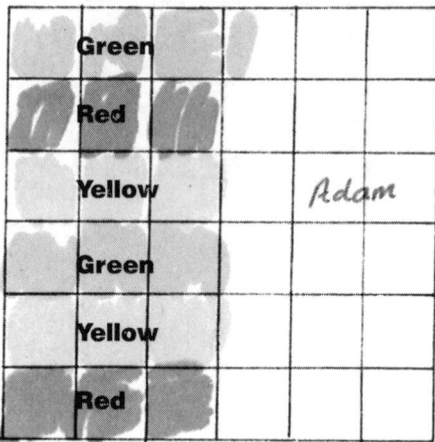

Figure 4.9 Adam's square.

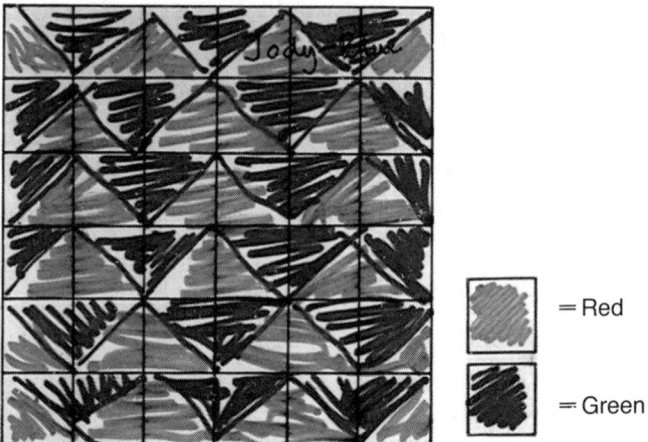

Figure 4.10 Jody-Blue's square of 'triangles'

there were three green sets but when I asked her to count them aloud she realised she had missed the single green square and that that gave her four sets. She decided that there were three red sets, pointing separately to the vertical line of two squares, the vertical line of six squares and the single square. I asked, 'You don't think this is just two sets?' to which she replied, 'No.'

She then went on to complete figure 4.12 which she said was 'A set of red and a set of yellow', I asked 'How many lines are there like this of yellow?', pointing to the left-hand vertical line of six yellow squares. Lianne replied, 'Three', without counting aloud. I continued, 'And of red?' to which

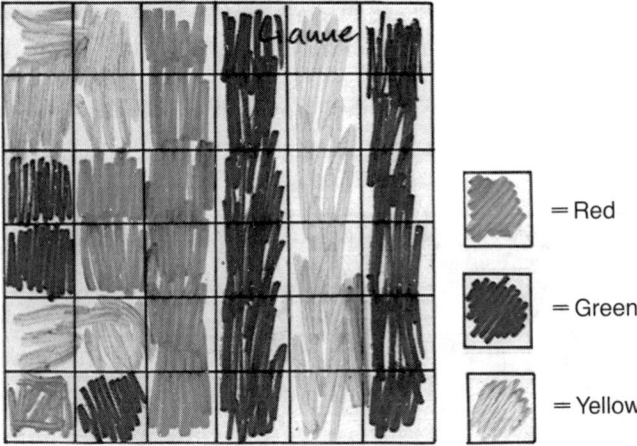

Figure 4.11 Lianne's first square

Figure 4.12 Lianne's second square

she again replied, 'Three'. Then I asked, 'How many lines are there like this yellow one?', pointing to the top horizontal line of three yellow squares. This time she counted, 'One, two, three, four, five, *six*'. I added, 'And of red?' to which she immediately replied, 'Six'. I enquired, 'How did you know the answer so quickly?' She said, 'Because there's six yellows.'

Two weeks later, when the group had reached a suitable stopping-point in another activity, Adam asked if they could 'Do those little mats again.' The rest seemed eager to do so as well and were delighted when I said that they could. Again they produced some interesting results but it would take too much space to discuss them all here. Hayley's examples seem worthy of particular note, however, since they brought a new line of thinking into play.

Hayley completed the squares shown in figure 4.13. She made various comments at various stages. For example, having just completed her second

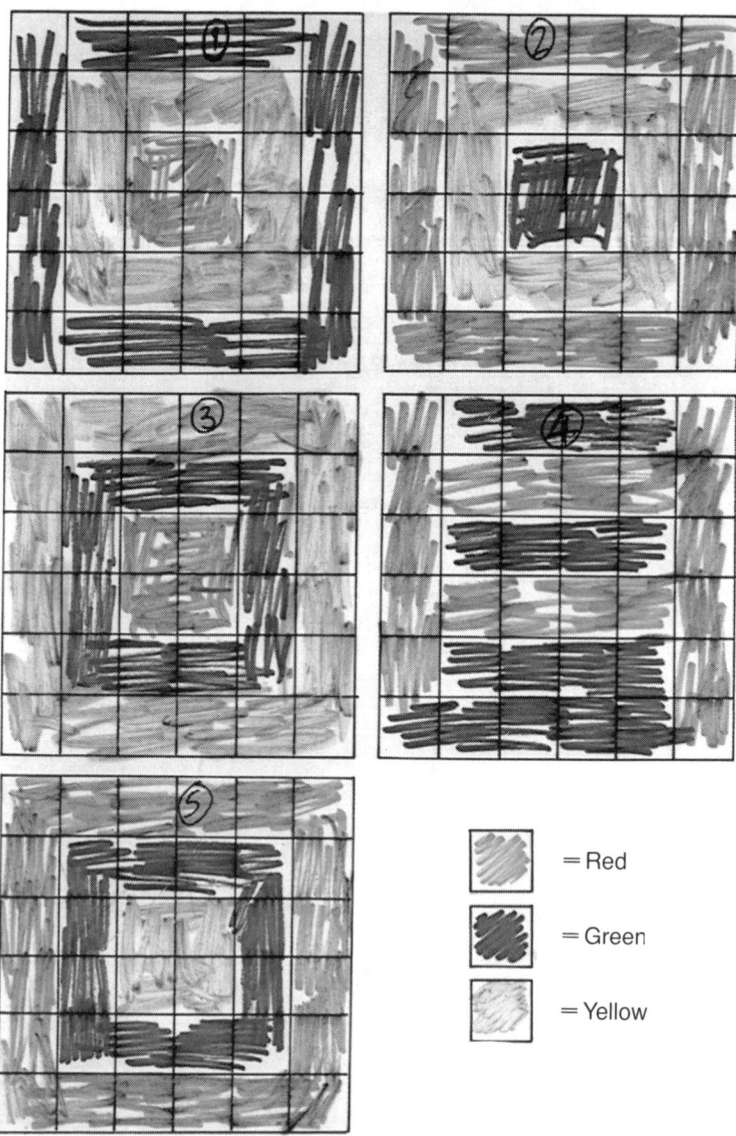

Red

Green

Yellow

Figure 4.13 Hayley's new ideas

square she said, 'It's nearly the same.' When asked how it was different, she replied that the first one was, 'Green, yellow, then red in the middle', whereas the second one was 'Red, yellow, then green.' It was interesting that her fourth example was quite different from the rest! Perhaps at that stage she thought she could not do any more like the other three – perhaps she perceived that she had used each of green, yellow and red for the outermost colours. At any rate, she returned to the theme to complete her fifth example.

Like the rest of the group, Hayley was keen for me to write numbers on the squares to show in which order she had completed them. She said which she had done 'first' and 'second'. I helped her vocalise the words 'third', 'fourth' and 'fifth'.

We had no more time left that day but it occurred to me that Hayley's work could form the stimulus to an activity with the rest of the group. I decided to try out the idea the following week. I started the group off by asking them to look at all the examples they had finished the previous week. Soon their attention became focused on Hayley's set of squares and they made various comments about them. These included Jody-Blue saying 'That's nearly the same as that one', referring to the first and second squares; 'And that's nearly the same as that one', referring to the second and third squares; 'And that's nearly the same as that one', referring to the third and fifth squares. When I asked how they were nearly the same, Jody-Blue commented that 'There's little bits in the middle coloured in', and 'There's a big square and a middle-sized square and a tiny one.'

I said I thought that all the group could have a go at making up some patterns like Hayley's but using a sheet with the squares drawn on it already, as in figure 4.14, to avoid them being distracted by the original

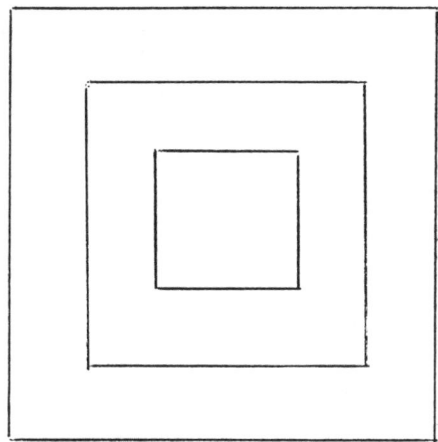

Figure 4.14 The new sheet based on Hayley's work

41

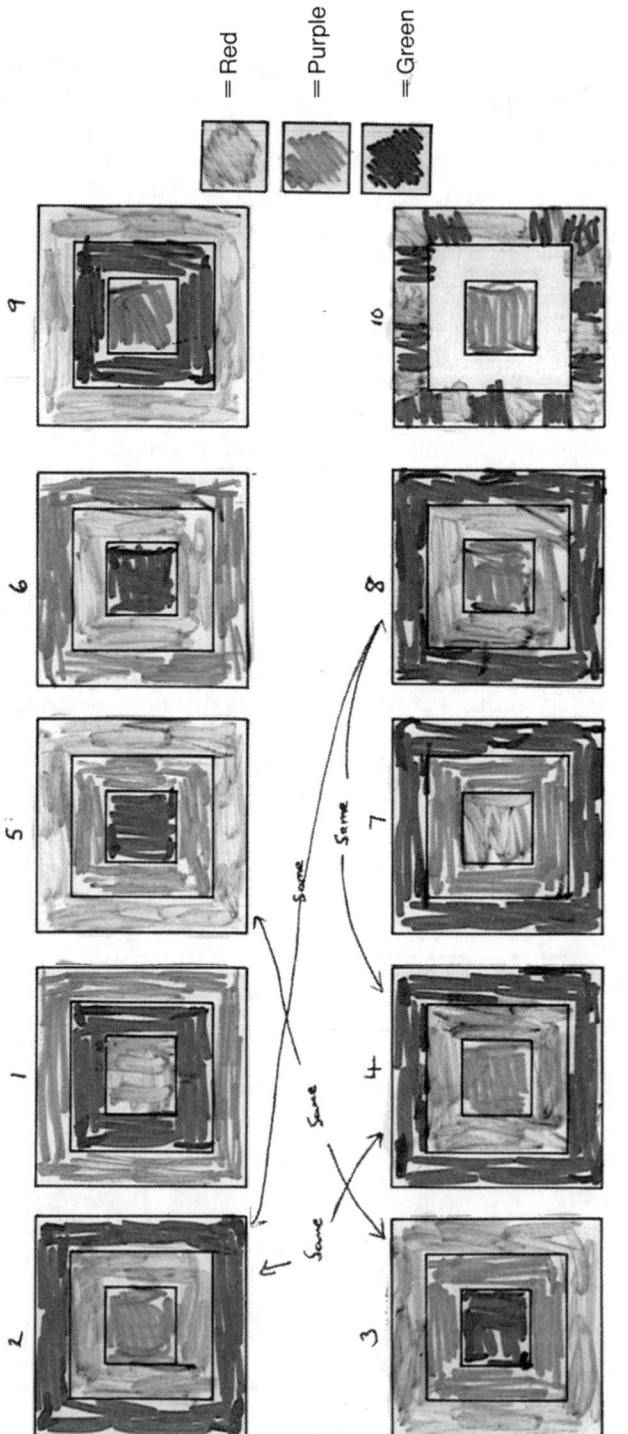

Figure 4.15 Alan's squares, showing his identification of identical squares

thirty-six tiny squares at this point. This time I gave them red, green and *purple* colouring pencils, so that Hayley might not feel she was doing exactly the same task again.

The children soon became involved in seeing how many different examples they could make. Alan succeeded in exhausting the possibilities, and several other children found five different ones. This was far from easy, particularly as the children could not put the examples side by side to compare them: they were fixed on one sheet. Several tried things like reversing the order of two colours from one square when completing another square.

Alan's work can be seen in figure 4.15. I wrote in the numerals as a result of his telling me in which order he had completed the squares. Together we spoke the ordinal numbers 'first', 'second', and 'third', etc. I also wrote in 'Same' and drew in the arrows as he pointed out identical pairs to me. Having finished his ninth example (which gave him the final square of the set of six possible ones using Hayley's rule), Alan seemed convinced that he could not complete any more. When I asked, 'Could you do any different ones?' he replied, 'If I had orange I could!'. He then went on to colour his tenth square, not keeping to the original rule. Other children also deviated from the rule when they thought they could not do any more of Hayley's kind of squares. In so deviating, Adam managed to exhaust the possibilities for a new type of frame. In each of his examples of this new type, he drew diagonal lines to connect the vertices of the outer square to the corresponding vertices of the middle square, thus creating four trapezia as shown in figure 4.16. In the first example, he drew the diagonal lines in red, coloured

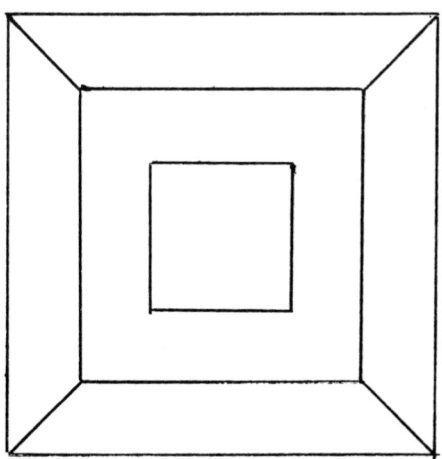

Figure 4.16 Adam's four trapezia

one opposite pair of trapezia in green and the other opposite pair in purple. In the second example, the diagonal lines were green with the pairs of trapezia in purple and red. In the third example, the diagonal lines were purple with the pairs of trapezia in red and green. Was he aware that it would be impossible to do any more?

5

NUMBER SQUARES

ORGANISATION

This was an activity with a group of four children: Vanessa (5.07), Ben (5.05), Anne-Marie (5.08) and Helen (5.03). The rest of the class were also working in small groups, on a variety of different ideas. I was circulating round the groups. A tape recorder was left on the table where Ben, Vanessa, Anne-Marie and Helen were.

ACTIVITY

To each of the four children I gave a small plastic bag containing a set of nine squares of card with dots on them as in figure 5.1. The squares were jumbled but the children's first reaction was to sort them into groups with the same number of dots on each square, commenting on the numbers of dots as they were doing this.

Anne-Marie arranged hers like that in figure 5.2. She commented, 'I've

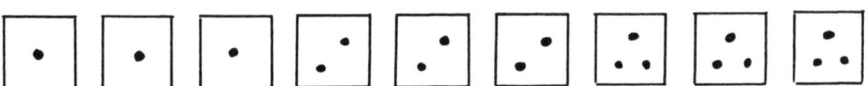

Figure 5.1 Each child was given a set of cards showing these patterns of dots

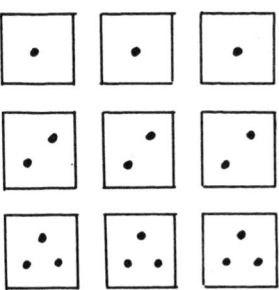

Figure 5.2 Anne-Marie's arrangement

45

done a set. They're in a line.' I said that it was strange that she should do that because I also had with me some grids into which arrangements like Anne-Marie's would fit and I gave the children a grid each drawn on paper, like the one in figure 5.3. The children made various comments about the grids. These included Helen saying 'squares' and Ben turning his paper round and saying, 'They look like diamonds.' Presumably framing a perception linked with Anne-Marie's earlier comment, Helen said, 'They're all in line.'

The group put their cards on to the squares. It was interesting to see how they structured this. Then, completely of her own accord, Anne-Marie started to copy the dots off her cards on to her grid, using a pencil. I commented that this was a good idea because she would be able to remember what she had done and I suggested that the others might do so too. I went off to talk with another group whilst they did that.

When I returned, the children were eager to tell me things about their grids, which they had filled in as shown in figure 5.4. I put Vanessa's completed grid in the middle of the table and asked them all how many dots there were altogether in the top line, moving my finger along the top row as I said this. They counted three. I asked the same question about the second and third lines, for which they counted six and nine. I suggested that they might all count their dots like this, making a note of the number at the side of each line of squares so that they could remember it, similar to the way in which Anne-Marie had found a way of remembering where the cards themselves were placed. I mentioned that they could use their number ladders if they were unsure how to write down the numbers they found. (These were pieces of card with 'ladders' drawn on them and the numerals 1 to 10 inserted in the spaces between the rungs, which the class teacher had given to each child.) I also suggested that they could then start again by arranging

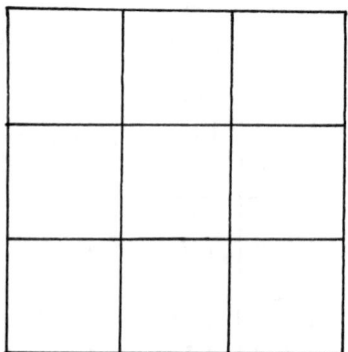

Figure 5.3 The grid

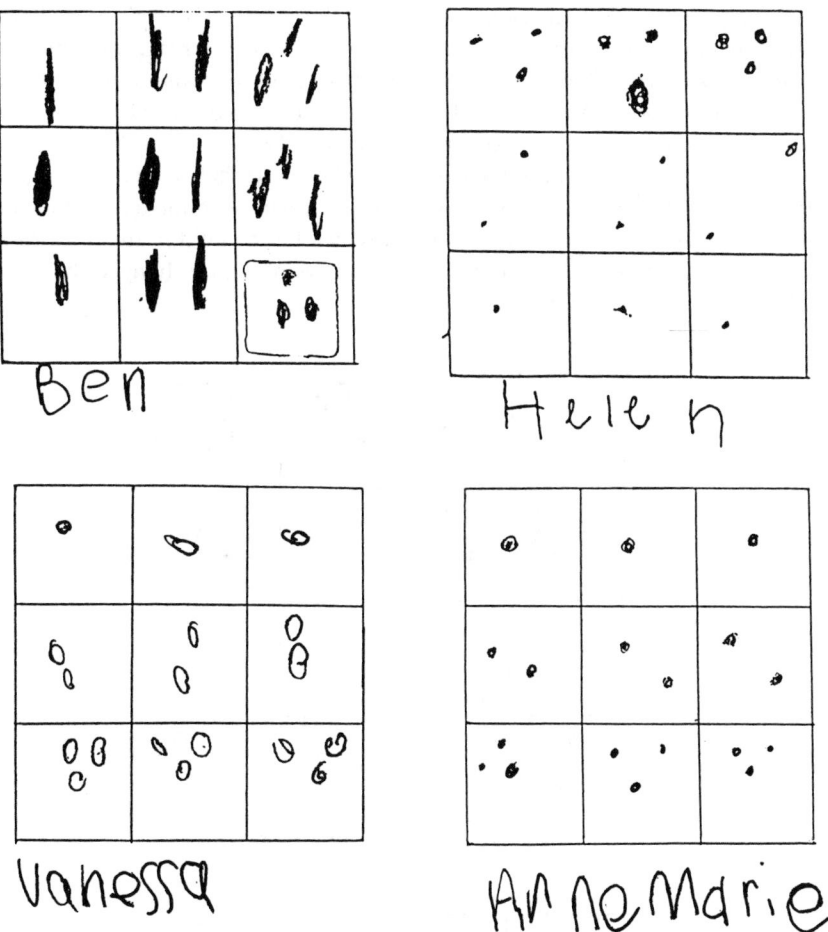

Figure 5.4 Examples of the children's work on the grids

their squares in a different way on a fresh grid and I left the children with a pile of blank grids in the centre of the table. I left the group.

When I came back, each of the children had written in the numbers on their first grids and were either working on or had completed their second grids. They were keen to talk about what they had done and their comments to me and those already on the tape recorder revealed a whole host of mathematical perceptions. As examples:

1 Ben was delighted that *each* of the rows of numbers in his first square came to six. He said that they were 'All the same number', and added, 'I didn't know I could make a six with a two, a three and a one!' He also

47

commented that he had 'Got two sixes' in his second example (see figure 5.5). I realised, however, that there must be something wrong with this as I knew it was impossible to have five, six, six as a set of totals. A quick glance at what Ben had done revealed that he had four lots of one dot instead of three. I decided to ask him how many one dots, two dots and three dots he had on his grid. He counted and showed some surprise at there being just two twos but four ones. To *my* surprise he realised immediately that he needed to switch a one dot to a two dot which he then did in the third row. Furthermore, apparently without any further counting, he changed the '6' to a '7', shown in figure 5.6.

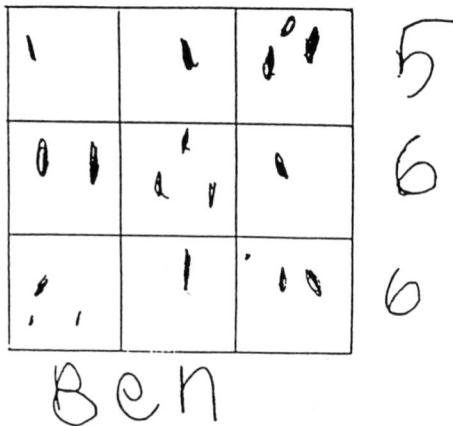

Figure 5.5 Ben's work on the grid

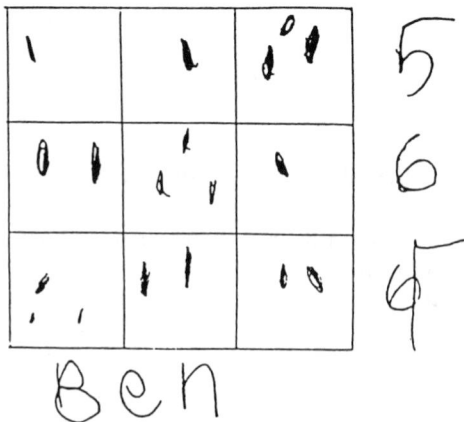

Figure 5.6 Ben's corrected grid

48

2   Helen had completed her first example by placing three threes along the top row, three twos along the middle row and three ones along the bottom row (see figure 5.4 again). For her second example, she put three dots, two dots, one dot along the top row, then repeated this for each of the other rows. When she looked at this afterwards, she was intrigued to find that what she had going across the paper in her first grid, now went down the paper in her second grid! She decided to write her original totals of nine, six, three along the bottom of the second grid. She also totalled the dots going across the bottom row and, having found that this gave six, said that the other rows would be six too. Furthermore, she counted to see how many dots she had on her grid *altogether*. She reached eighteen correctly and wrote the numerals for this, also correctly, at the side of her grid (see figure 5.7).

I then took out some sets of blank squares of card and put them in front of the children. They were excited by these and asked if they could put on their own dots. This they set about doing. I left the group again.

After a while, Ben called over to me whilst I was working with an adjacent group of children and said, 'I need one more piece of paper.' When I asked why he replied, 'I want to do all the numbers the same number.' When I asked him to explain further he added, 'One one, two twos, three threes, four fours!' I gave him an extra little square of card and asked him where he would put it. Referring to his grid he said he would draw 'one more square.' I left him to it. Later I found that he had arranged his squares

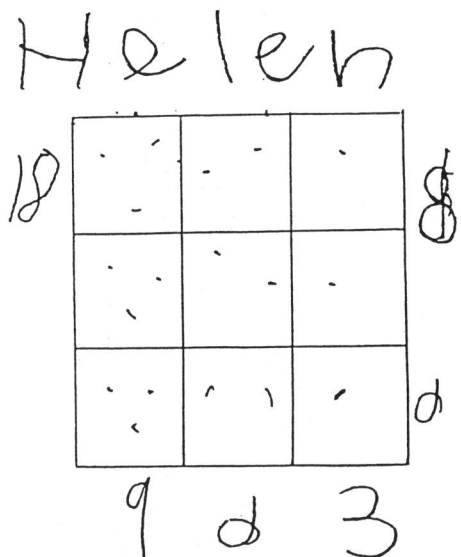

Figure 5.7 Helen's grid

49

as in figure 5.8. The tape recorder revealed a problem when he came to seeing how many dots he had in the row of three fours. He counted to twelve correctly and announced in a triumphant voice to Vanessa, 'Do you know how much I've got in that one? Twelve!' but then added less enthusiastically, 'I don't know how to write a twelve!' Vanessa did, however, and showed Ben '12' to which he exclaimed, 'Twelve? That doesn't look like a twelve! A twelve is more than a one and a two, I bet it is!' whereupon he came over to me and asked me how to write it. I went to fetch a number ladder which went past '10' so that he could count for himself and find '12' on it. In the mean time, Ben had helped himself to a ruler and was busy counting along the numerals on it when I returned. On reaching '12' he exclaimed in amazement, 'It *is* a one and a two!' I commented that this was, indeed, rather strange and that we ought to find out more about it another time. (On a subsequent occasion I referred to this incident, using the children's recollections of it, to start off some activities concerned with place-value.) Ben was intrigued by the other numbers on this longer number ladder (it went up to '22') and talked about such things as there being lots of numbers with a '1' in them; then he pointed out each '2' in '20', '21' and '22'; and guessed how the next few numbers would be written.

The other children also seemed to gain a lot from making up and working with their own cards. Some of their grids are shown in figure 5.9. Points worthy of note about these particular examples include:

1   Helen had again chosen to have three of each of her numbers and to keep the numbers in sequence. The '12' over the top of the '11' is her own correction. She knew how to write those numerals unaided, also '15' and

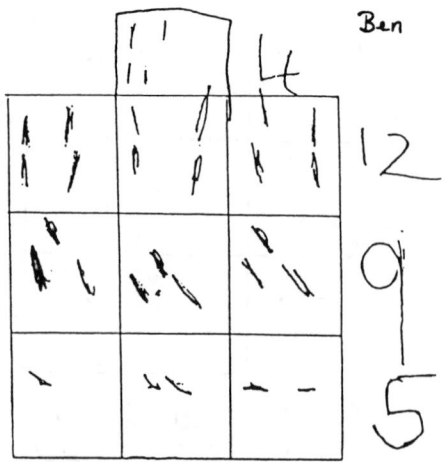

Figure 5.8 Ben's grid, showing his 'extra' square

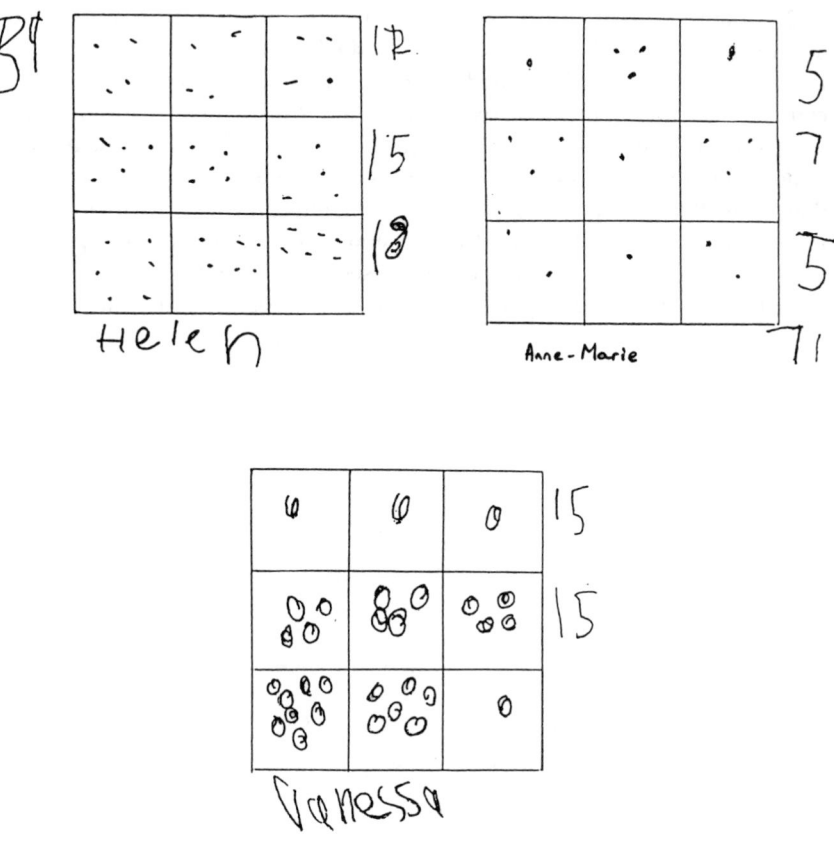

Figure 5.9 A selection of the children's own cards

'18'. The '39' was her record of an attempt to work out the total number of dots on the grid. It is not correct but that seems insignificant when viewed alongside the fact that here is a five year old perfectly willing to set about trying to count what must have looked like a great many dots!

2   Anne-Marie had retained the idea of having one dot, two dots and three dots, but has changed the number of one dots and two dots. She put her cards in the grid in a symmetrical pattern. Like Helen, she also set about finding the *total* number of dots and did so correctly. She then counted along Ben's big number ladder to see how to write seventeen and found the correct numeral. Again, the fact that she transposed the figures when recording the number seems a minor detail when compared to the rest of the task she set herself. She wrote the numerals in the order that she said 'seven-teen': this, of course, was actually very sensible!

51

3   Vanessa drew the dots on her grids without putting any on the squares of card. When I first saw her grid she had written just one '15' on it, the one by the side of the middle row. I thought that perhaps she had counted the three fours incorrectly but when I asked her to tell me about what she had done her comments revealed that she had counted the number of dots in both the top and middle rows. I expressed some surprise and said that I had thought, wrongly, that the '15' referred to just the middle row. Immediately, she wrote on the other '15' and said that this was to help me see what she meant! It is also interesting to see that her dots in the third row total fifteen as well and to ponder whether she made this so on purpose.

6

CHRISTMAS TREES

ORGANISATION

Seven children worked on this activity at various points throughout the day whilst others were carrying out other things. I started them off at three separate points as they finished other activities. At the end of the afternoon some of the group talked to the rest of the class about what they had done.

The children were: Claire (5.02), Maria (5.02), Andrew (5.07), Louise (5.04), Lucy (5.03), Daniel (5.06) and Sara (5.02). These children were the ones whose 'number work' was giving the class teacher the greatest cause for concern. I left a tape recorder on the table where the children came and sat in turn.

ACTIVITY

At the start of each episode with the different children I gave them each an outline drawing, supposed to be a Christmas tree, together with trays of little paper circles, triangles and squares which I said they could colour in red or blue and stick on the 'trees' as 'decorations'. (The children had been working with circles, triangles and squares from the class logic-blocks so there was a connection between this activity and earlier work.)

I asked the children to think carefully about which shapes they were using. For example, to one small group I said, 'When you're choosing them, don't just do any old thing, really think hard about what you want. Look at your tree and decide what you want and look at these [shapes] and decide what you're going to use.'

The children named the shapes when they saw them. Claire even anticipated my actions – I had put the circles, then the triangles on the table and she said, 'The next ones are squares, I bet!' She was delighted to find that they were.

With the exceptions of Maria and Andrew, all the children were able to continue the activity without help from me, but when I had the opportunity to do so I asked individuals to talk about what they were doing and asked them questions. Andrew was distracted several times (this was usual) and had to be reminded to continue with his task. I decided at one point to talk to Maria about her work because, having coloured in some of her shapes, she stuck them on her tree back to front.

The children's responses to such questions as, 'What can you say about your tree?' were interesting, as also was observing how they had arranged their shapes and trying to surmise how much of the apparent structuring was intentional. Some details follow:

Louise

Louise put one of each of the three sorts of shapes along both sides of her tree (see figure 6.1). That this was intentional became apparent when one of the shapes was blown on the floor before she had stuck them on. She was convinced it was a triangle which was missing, because she had a circle and a square left on that side.

Referring to her combinations of triangles and squares at the foot of the tree, Louise said, 'There's two presents', and went on to explain that the triangles were bows. Before putting the uppermost triangle on the right hand present she counted the blue shapes and the red shapes quietly and then announced, 'I've got five blues and seven reds.' I asked how many she had altogether, for which she recounted and arrived at twelve correctly. She called her circle at the top 'a gingerbread man' – she had apparently made one in cookery recently. I noted that her 'gingerbread man' circle had both colours on it but that she had counted it just once, in with the red shapes. I asked, 'Why did you count that as a red one and not as a blue one?' to which she replied, 'Because it's got red lips on.'

Andrew

Andrew put shapes on just one side of his tree at first. When I asked him what he could say about it he replied, 'I haven't got much money.' Puzzled, I asked him what he meant. He said that he only had enough money to buy a few decorations! Later, however, he decided he had some more money and could put on more shapes!

He ended up with one shape on each spoke (see figure 6.2). Spontaneously he counted the shapes and told me that he had three squares, two circles and two triangles but this did not fit with what I could see. I thought perhaps he had counted incorrectly, but when I asked him to show me how he had counted the shapes, it emerged that he was calling the squares 'circles' and vice-versa. I talked with him about this. When Andrew himself talked to the rest of the class at the end of the afternoon about what he had done, he chose to mention the numbers of the different shapes again and

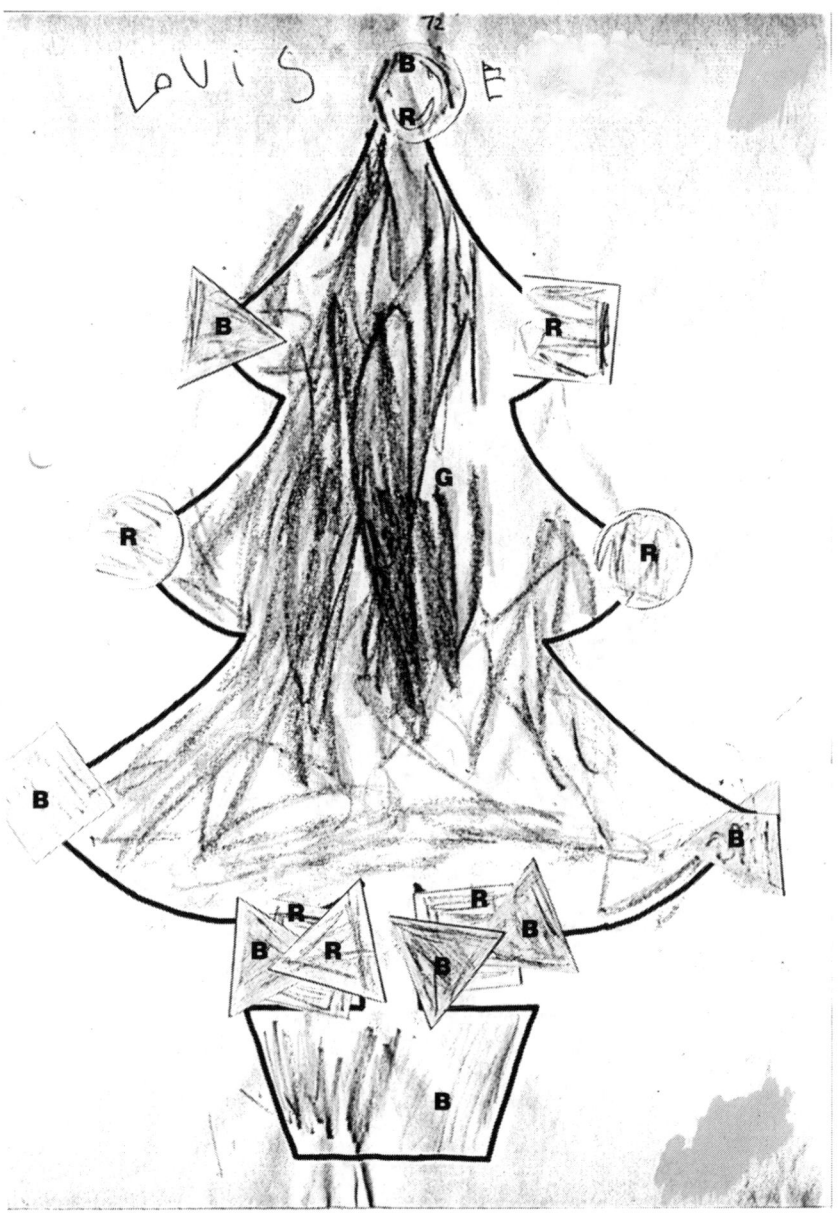

G = Green
R = Red
B = Blue

Figure 6.1 Louise's Christmas tree

G = Green
R = Red
B = Blue

Figure 6.2 Andrew's Christmas tree

this time he used the words 'squares' and 'circles' correctly.

At one point, Andrew also commented to me that he had one red circle, one blue circle, one red triangle, one blue triangle, one red square and one blue square. Thus he had exhausted the possibilities! I noted that he had not included the shape at the top of the tree in his reckoning and I asked him about it. He said, 'Oh, that's the fairy!' as if it therefore did not count!

Maria

Maria's was perhaps the most careless-looking of all the completed trees in that her crayoning was rather haphazard, often going off the edges of her shapes. However, she had certainly structured what she did and was able to make comments about it. She had chosen to put only squares on the spokes and talked about putting one on each. Also, she commented that all her squares were blue and all her circles were red. (She had put three circles on the tree itself and one on the base.)

Claire

Claire put on just four shapes but took particular care colouring these and the rest of the tree. I had suggested that the children coloured their trees when they had finished decorating them, to make them look more realistic.

When asked what she could say about what she had done, she counted all the shapes 'One, two, three, four.' I asked, 'Can you tell me anything else about them if you count them?' She said, 'There's two squares and two circles', and added, 'They're the same side' (pointing to the blue shapes) 'and they're the same side' (pointing to the red shapes). She also explained that the squares were presents and that one of the circles was a decoration and the other a fairy!

Lucy

As she was doing it, Lucy commented about putting three triangles at the top of her tree and then she talked of having a triangle, a square and a circle down the centre of the tree (see figure 6.3).

Having finished putting on the decorations, she said, 'I've got one red and three ... four blue.' I asked how many that was altogether. She counted aloud and arrived at five correctly.

Daniel

Having originally arranged his three shapes at the foot of the tree like that in figure 6.4. Daniel called out to me excitedly, 'I've made a triangle!' He added, 'It's a pattern ... that's a pattern of a triangle!' When he actually

G = Green
R = Red
B = Blue

Figure 6.3 Lucy's Christmas tree

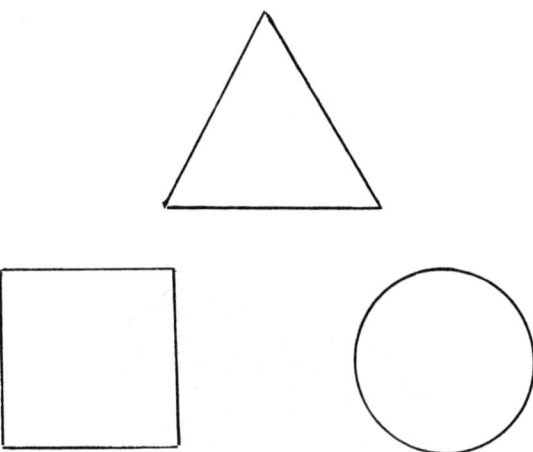

Figure 6.4 Daniel's original arrangement of shapes at the foot of his Christmas tree

stuck on the shapes, however, he moved the circle a little and said 'Now it's not quite a triangle at the bottom' (see figure 6.5). I made a mental note that he ought to become involved in some activities where not all the triangles were equilateral ones! He also perceived that his top three shapes made a triangle too.

When he had finished his tree, Daniel said to me 'There's only one blue.' I asked him how many reds he had. He counted quietly and arrived at five. I continued, 'So how many altogether?' He counted up to six aloud and said, 'Six together'.

Sara

As can be seen from figure 6.6, Sara made a pattern of triangles down the centre of her tree. She told me she was doing 'Red, blue, red, blue' and answered correctly which colour would come next when I asked her at one point. Having finished the centre line, she counted the blue and the red triangles in it and seemed highly amused that the numbers were the same! Then she wanted to count the shapes altogether and asked me to help her. I imagine this was because she was unsure of some of the number words. Together we counted up to twelve. She seemed delighted to have reached what to her was such a big number.

The tape recorder picked up many incidental remarks which the children made whilst I was away from them. Some of these were nothing to do with the activity itself and not mathematical. Others were concerned with the shapes the children were choosing and some referred to such things as the

B = Blue
R = Red
G = Green

Figure 6.5 Daniel's Christmas tree

R = Red
B = Blue
G = Green

Figure 6.6 Sara's Christmas tree

61

number of children at the table; the number of coloured pencils, etc. For example, seeing the heap of blue and red pencils in front of them at the beginning, Lucy said, 'We could have two each', to which Louise continued 'One blue one and one red one', and Daniel commented on there being 'lots of reds' and 'lots of blues'.

7

PLATES OF BISCUITS

BACKGROUND/ORGANISATION

The class teacher had given all the children some sheets like that shown in figure 7.1. For each line of the sheet, the children had to work out how many 'biscuits' there were on each of the two 'plates', write the numeral in the space underneath, then work out how many 'biscuits' that would be altogether and put that numeral in the right hand space. On a previous occasion, the children had completed some similar sheets but there had then been a large circle on the right hand side of each pair of 'plates', to act as a larger plate.

I suggested that, on another occasion, the teacher could try giving the children *blank* circles, inviting them to make up their own examples. This she did, with very interesting results, two of which can be seen as figures 7.2 and 7.3.

I decided to try to develop some further activities using the children's own generated sheets. I photocopied some of them on to larger paper, leaving some space for further recording, and inserted a number ladder. The development of those pieces shown as figures 7.2 and 7.3 is described below. Ilona (5.05), Matthew (5.06) and Sam (5.04) worked on these particular pieces. Unfortunately, Jemma was absent and so could not continue with or comment about her own piece.

A tape recorder was left on the table where Ilona, Matthew and Sam were working.

ACTIVITY

I commented to Matthew, Ilona and Sam that I had been looking at some work they had been doing with their class teacher and referred to the fact that they had made up their own sheets. Producing Ilona's example (as in figure 7.2), I continued, 'Some of the things you did were very interesting. I'm interested in Ilona's here because of the way she's chosen the numbers.'

63

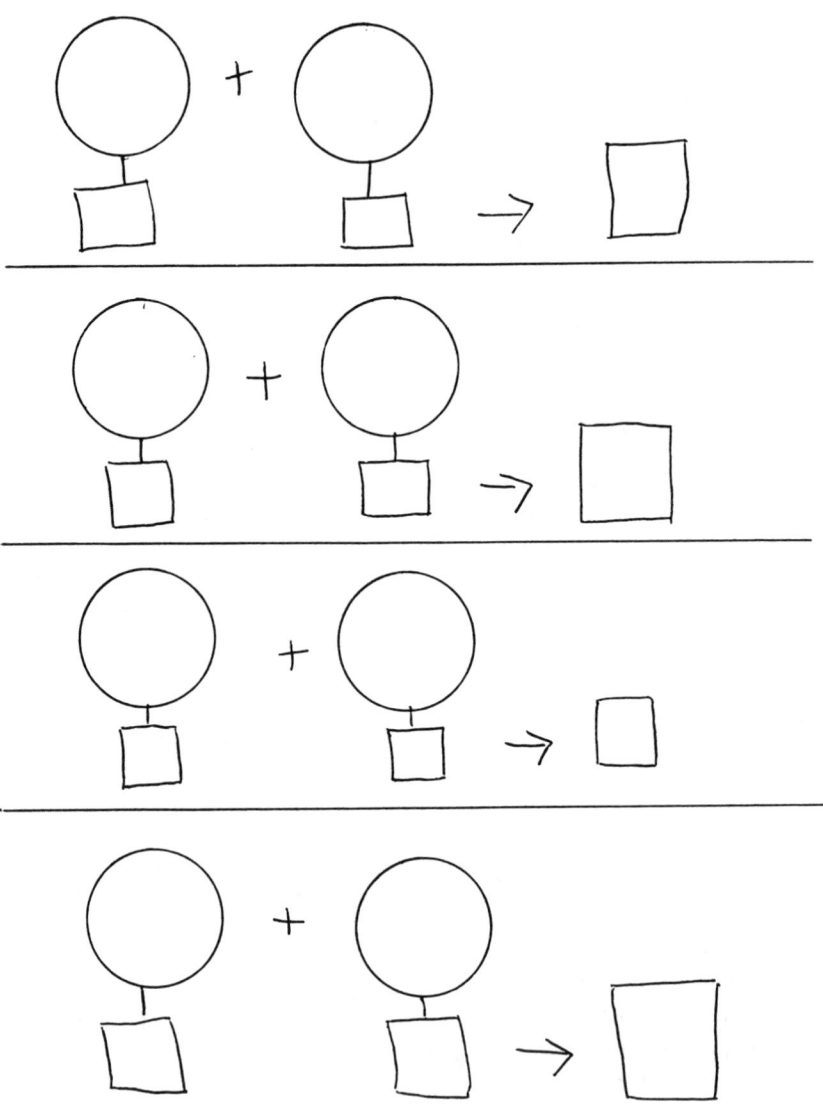

Figure 7.1 The basic sheet

Looking at the sheet, Matthew said, 'One, one; two, two; three, three; four, four;' and the other two started to join in with him. Matthew then continued, 'One and one makes two; two and two makes four; three and three makes six;' and Sam added, 'Four and four makes eight.' I asked what was special about the numbers. The children did not respond. I thought perhaps this was because what I had in mind, namely that the numbers were the

64

Figure 7.2 Ilona's work

same, was too 'obvious' a remark for them to make as they had already indicated the equivalence in the way they read out the numbers in pairs. So I supplied what I had been looking for, saying, 'She's chosen the same.' They seemed to agree with this but Matthew added, 'Except they're different colours!' (Ilona had coloured in the objects in her circles in a

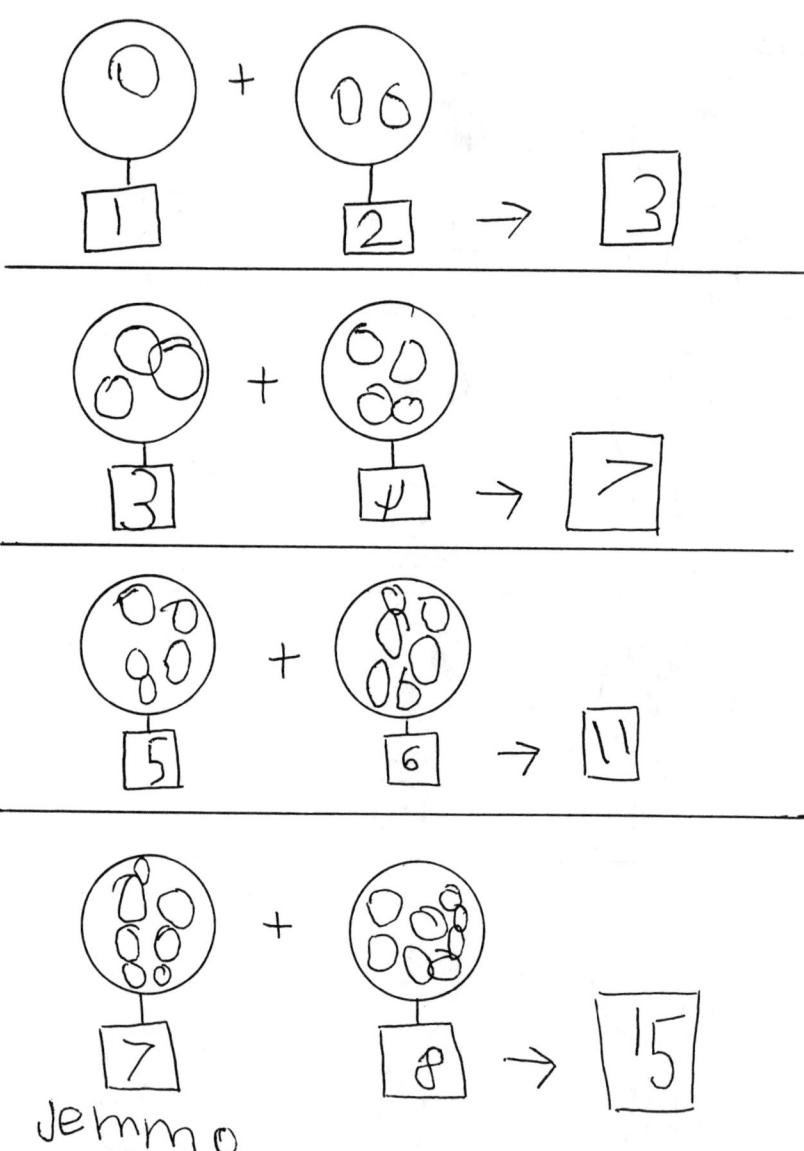

Figure 7.3 Jemma's work

variety of colours.) Sam also pointed out that Ilona had written the numeral for two in different ways. Pointing to the 'ς' in '1 + 1 → ς ' and to the first '2' in '2 + 2 → 4', Matthew said, 'That two's facing that way and that two's facing that way.' I asked how we would normally write it and Sam pointed to the correct one. Interpreting that Ilona looked rather uncomfortable, I said to her that what mattered most was that we had recognised both.

I then showed the children photocopies of Ilona's work which I had made. They were intrigued by these. They commented on such things as the number ladder being on the sheet as well and that everything was in black, not in colours. I said that they were all going to work on Ilona's to start with and gave out one sheet to each child. Ilona looked quite pleased at this idea!

I asked the children to read out the 'answers' from Ilona's paper. This they did: 'Two, four, six, eight.' I then invited them to find these numbers on their number ladders and to put a mark by the side of them. Ilona seemed delighted when she found the first one!

After the children had marked their ladders, I said, 'Have a look at where those numbers are. What do you notice about them?' Sam replied, 'It's left one number.' I asked the others if they saw what Sam meant and their responses suggested that they did. I said, 'So it goes two, miss a number, four, miss a number, six, miss a number, eight', and continued, 'Where would it go next, do you think, if we were to put another dot on?' Matthew and Sam both said 'Ten.' I invited all three children to put a mark by the '10' and to keep going 'marking where the numbers would go next'. This they did. I commented, 'That's a guess, isn't it, at where those numbers will go?'

When the children had finished, I asked, 'Could you pick one of those numbers that you've marked and then think how we could make a sum that would give us that number?' As I was saying this I realised it was likely to be incomprehensible and the children's lack of response seemed to confirm this. So I decided to be more specific and suggested they started with the number they had marked first after eight, which was ten. I asked if they had any ideas for two numbers which would make ten. I was surprised by the quick and correct responses: Matthew said, 'Five and five', and Sam said, 'Or four and six!' Sam's idea, of course, did not consist of two numbers the same, but I did not wish to dampen his response by drawing his attention to it at that point. In any case, when I listened to the tape afterwards, I realised my request did not require equal sets at all. I asked if the boys' ideas would work and when Sam and Matthew said they would I asked, 'Can you be certain?' Matthew said 'You could have a piece of paper and try.' I suggested that he and Sam did so.

I decided to talk with Ilona because I guessed that she was not clear what was happening. I said, 'They're trying to make that ten by putting those two numbers together like you did. You had three and three, four and four ... What would you guess at to make ten?' She said 'Four and four.' I asked 'Now four and four made what?' Ilona replied, 'Eight.' I said, 'So it won't be four and four ... what do you think would be a good guess?' She suggested 'Six and six', which I invited her to try.

In the meantime, Matthew had drawn two sets of five blobs, counted them together and found that they did indeed give ten. I asked if he would like to guess at another number. Pointing to the '16' on the number ladder he said, 'That one.' I commented that this was sixteen and asked what he thought might make it. He started to work something out on his fingers.

Sam said that four and six also made ten. Like Matthew he had checked this by drawing two sets of blobs and counting them. Interestingly enough he had also inserted a '+' sign between the two sets. I asked if the six and the four would fit in with Ilona's pattern of one, one; two, two; three, three; four, four. He realised that it would not. I stressed that there was nothing wrong with what he had done, he was just not keeping the numbers the same.

Matthew suddenly exclaimed 'Twenty-eight!' I asked him what was twenty-eight. He said he thought sixteen and sixteen would be twenty-eight, no thirty-eight. I had thought that he was trying to *make* sixteen with a pair of equal numbers (perhaps he was originally?) but it now appeared that he was thinking what he would obtain from putting two sixteens together (and it seems worthy of note that his idea of twenty-eight or thirty-eight was a good estimate). Whilst talking with the others, I noticed Matthew drawing more blobs and counting them. Eventually he claimed, 'Makes thirty-two!' I asked if thirty-two was on the number ladder and he said it was not. I commented that he would certainly need a bigger number ladder to find it! I asked him if he might like to write it on his sheet instead. To my surprise he said he knew how to do this. Actually he wrote the numerals for thirty-two back to front but I did not want to lessen his obvious satisfaction by mentioning that minor detail at that point. Similarly, the fact that he wrote the numerals above his blobs for working out five and five seemed irrelevant too. See figure 7.4 for Matthew's completed sheet.

Meanwhile, Ilona had found that six and six gave twelve, not ten. She seemed quite disappointed by this but cheered up when she realised that twelve was also a marked number on her ladder. I asked her how she might show that the two sets of six blobs that she had drawn went with the twelve and not the ten. She drew a line around all the blobs and another one connecting this combined set to the '12' on the number ladder. I asked if she thought she could still try to get ten and reasserted that it could not be four and four as that gave eight, nor six and six as that gave twelve. I left her to think whilst I was talking with Sam and Matthew. A little later she called out excitedly 'Five and five! Five and five!' and set about trying this out. She was delighted to find that it worked. Of her own accord she drew round this second pair of sets of blobs and joined them to the '10' on the number ladder. See figure 7.5 for Ilona's completed sheet.

Whilst I was talking with Ilona and Matthew, Sam had decided to continue finding other pairs of numbers which gave ten. He worked them out in this order: four and six (as described above); three and seven; two and eight; one and nine; nought and ten; but recorded the last line above the rest because he had run out of room at the bottom of his sheet.

I was amazed at this completion of his self-imposed task **and** wondered

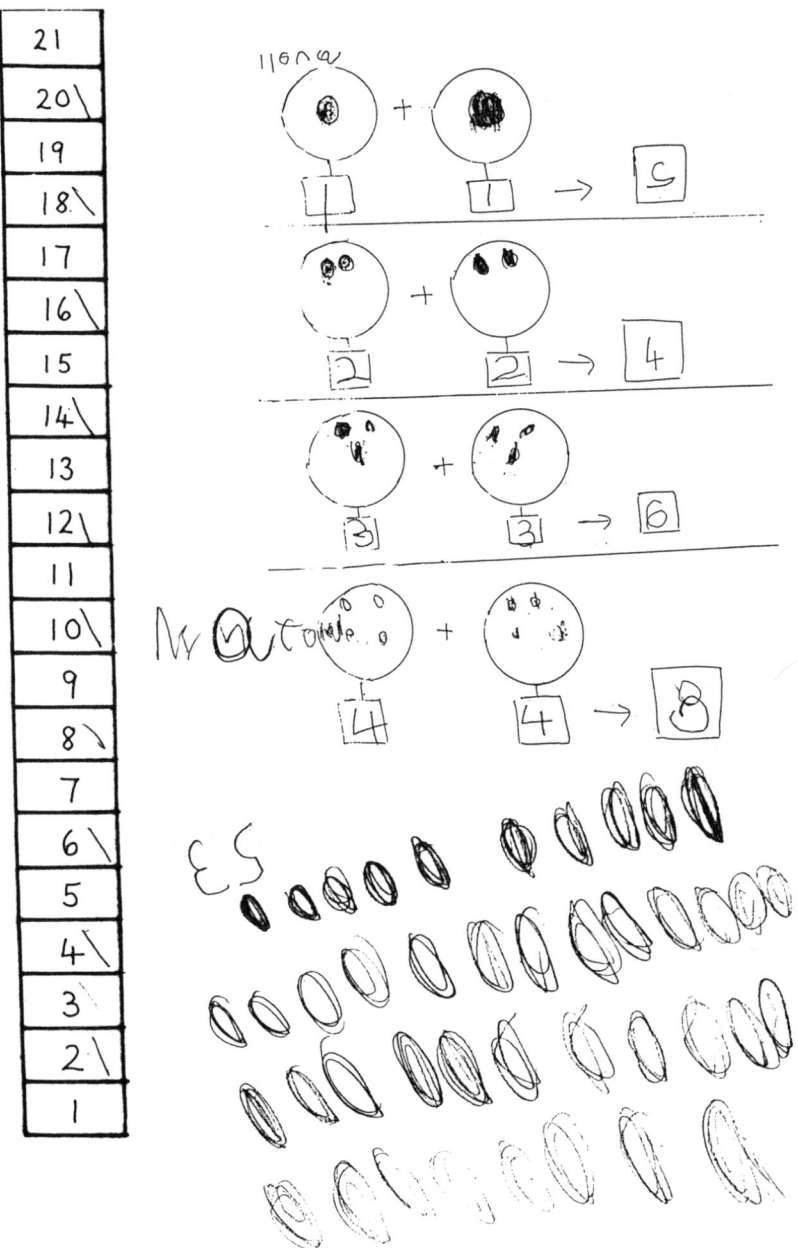

Figure 7.4 **Matthew's** completed sheet, based on Ilona's earlier work

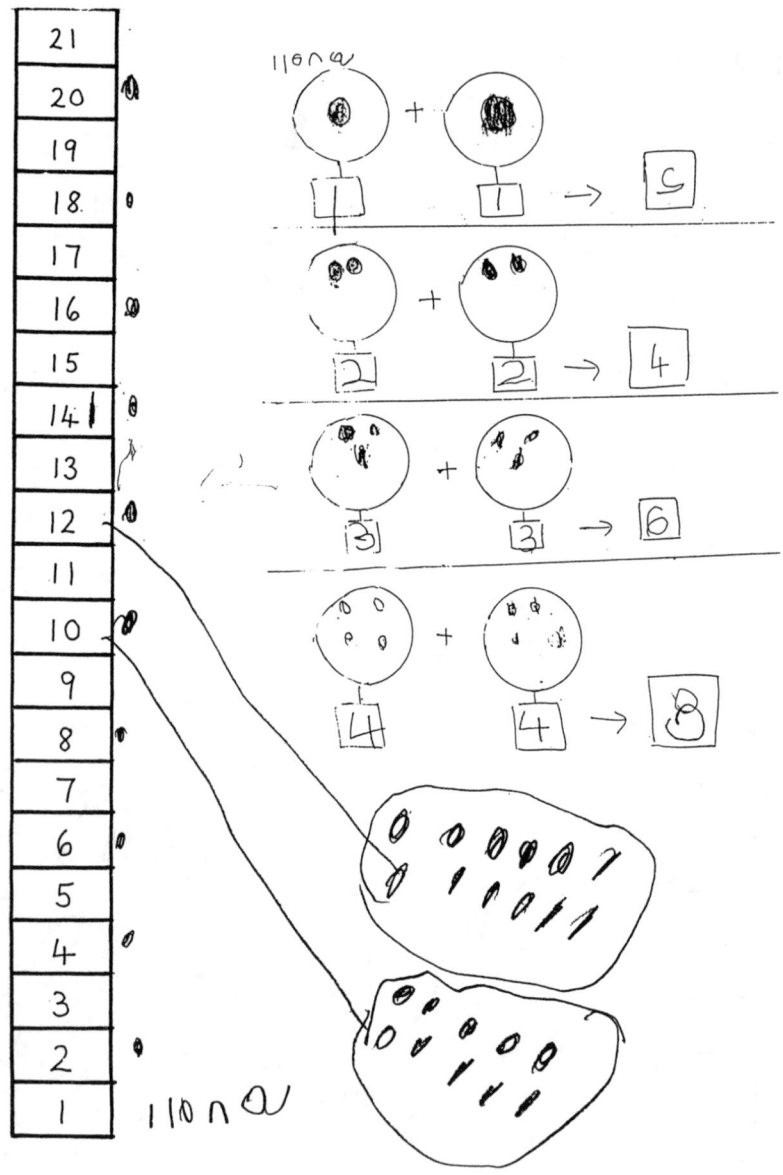

Figure 7.5 Ilona's completed sheet

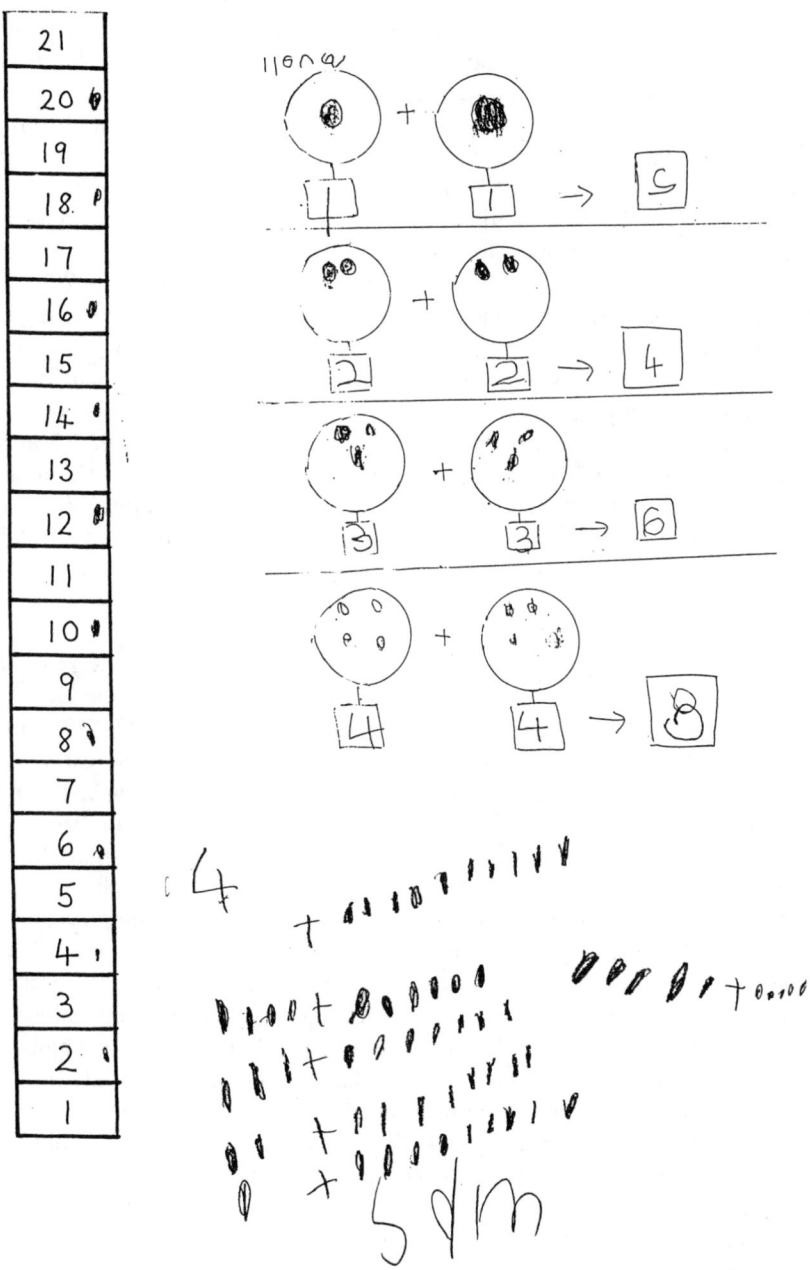

Figure 7.6 Sam's completed sheet

71

how much system he was building in on purpose and what he perceived in what he had completed. He also recorded the blobs for five and five but away from the other sets, and it is interesting to speculate why that was so. See figure 7.6 for Sam's completed sheet.

I said we could look at someone else's sheet from before and took out Jemma's. Matthew wanted to use his but I had not photocopied that one. I explained that this was not because his was not 'good', it was, but we had used some of Matthew's and Sam's work on other occasions and so we were using Ilona's and Jemma's 'for a change'.

I asked what we could say about Jemma's numbers (see figure 7.3 again). Matthew said, 'She did one, two, three, four, five, six, seven, eight.' I repeated this in pairs: 'So she did one, two; three, four; five, six; seven, eight.' I asked what was special about these numbers, to which Matthew responded, 'They come after each other.' I asked what her 'answers' were and Matthew and Sam read out, 'Three, seven, eleven, fifteen.' Matthew and Ilona then took some delight in repeating, 'Seven, eleven' several times, presumably attracted by the rhyme in them. I gave out copies of Jemma's papers and suggested they found her numbers on the number ladder. Whilst marking on hers, Ilona pointed to the '15' and exclaimed 'That one's the biggest number!'

I asked what the children could say about the numbers this time. Were they in a pattern? Ilona said that they were but Sam said they were not and went on to explain his thinking. Pointing to the '1' and '2' at the foot of his ladder he said 'Two'; then to the '4', '5', '6' 'Three'; the '8', '9', '10' 'Three'; and the '12', '13', '14' 'Three'. I commented that that was interesting then: *two* at the bottom, but then *three* between the dots. I suggested that we forgot about the two at the bottom and just thought about the threes between the dots themselves: where did the children think that the next marked number would be? Ilona said 'High' (!) and Matthew claimed 'Nineteen'. I asked 'How on earth do you think we could try and get nineteen doing what Jemma was doing which was to use numbers which are next to each other?' and repeated her pairings of numbers: 'One and two; three and four; five and six; seven and eight.' Matthew immediately said 'Nine and ten' and I invited them to try it. Each drew a set of nine blobs and a set of ten blobs and set about counting them. They seemed pleased to find that they did come up with nineteen. Again Ilona drew a pencil line around her sets of blobs and connected it to the numeral. Matthew commented that they could not do any more 'Because there's no space' (on the number ladder) which was indeed true!

Sam then commented that the nine and ten gave eighteen, not nineteen. Puzzled (because Sam had already said that it was nineteen and, in any case, he seemed such a competent counter), I asked, 'Shall we have a look at that, then? Sam makes it different, he doesn't make it nineteen, he makes it eighteen.' Ilona suggested, 'Perhaps he's done too many' (!) and I asked

Sam if that was what he thought. With a grin he said, 'No' and proceeded to show us how he had arrived at eighteen: his pencil was hiding one of the blobs! The others found this amusing and so did I: Sam was normally such a reserved, eager-to-do-everything-right sort of boy. Ilona started to re-count Sam's blobs, but while she was concentrating on this Sam drew on an extra one, so with much surprise Ilona arrived at twenty! Laughing, I asked Sam what had happened and he pointed to the extra blob. Matthew commented, 'He's got too much!' and I added, 'He's playing a game with us!'

8

A STICK OF CUBES

ORGANISATION

This was a ten-minute activity with a group of children: Cirwyn (5.00), Joseph (4.10), Leanne (5.00) and Xanthe (4.10). It formed the start of a session for this group. We were sitting in a corner of the room on a carpet. A tape recorder was on the floor as well.

ACTIVITY

I had joined four blue and three white unifix cubes together (as in figure 8.1), but put a '6' hat on the stick instead of a '7'.

(*I held the stick up in front of the chidren.*)

          MB: I'd like you to have a look at this. (*Something inaudible was said, then:*)

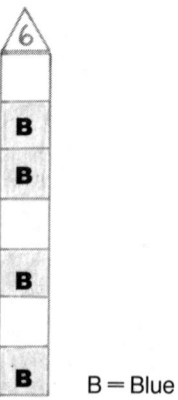

Figure 8.1 The stick of cubes

Cirwyn, Joseph, Six, Six, Six, Six, Six. (*each calling out 'Six' [somebody*
Xanthe, Leanne: *twice!], presumably looking at the number on the hat.*)
Joseph: Is there six blocks? (*Pause.*)
MB: Would you like to see, Joseph? (*I handed Joseph the stick.*)
Joseph: One, two, three, four, five, six, *seven*? (*putting his finger on each cube as he counted*) There's more than six, isn't there?
Xanthe: Seven. You've got to take one off.
MB: We've got to take one off, have we?
Xanthe: The blue one. Then there'd be the right number: six.
MB: Would you like to take that off, then, Joseph: the blue one that Xanthe's talking about?
Xanthe: Then there'd be six. (*Joseph took the last blue cube off the stick.*)
Joseph: One, two, three, four, five, six. She's quite right. So there is *six*.
MB: So it was wrong before?
Xanthe: Yes ... to start off with.
MB: Can you tell me anything else about it? (*taking the stick from Joseph*)
Joseph: There's white, blue ... two blues ... but white, blue, blue, white, blue, white (*reading from the hat downwards and correcting himself as he went*), and if you put the blue at the end there would be ... blue ... and then we could put just a blank one.
MB: Just a blank one? Where do you mean a blank one?
Joseph: Right at the end of the blue.
MB: So you want me to put this blue back on?
Joseph: Yes and then we could put a blank one there. (*pointing to the space beyond the end of the stick once I had put the blue cube back on*)
MB: What do you mean by a 'blank' one?
Xanthe: Black one.
Joseph: No colour ... just black.
MB: Black?
Joseph: Yes.
Xanthe: Yes, so that's the dead end.
MB: Why do you want to have one with a dead end on it?
Xanthe: 'Cos then there'd be the right number ... 'cos we don't count ...
Joseph: (*Interrupting.*) Without that on ... (*pointing to the last blue*) there'd be the right number ... with the blue

75

        ... without this on ... because the black you see we don't count in.

MB: So you mean we'd have a black on here? (*taking the last blue cube off again*)

Xanthe: Yes ... and we don't count the black one.

Joseph: Just count those. (*moving his finger along in the air by the rest of the cubes*)

MB: Oh, I see! Well, if we just kept it like this (*see figure 8.2*). I wonder if Leanne could tell us something else about what we've got here?

Joseph: (*Whispering.*) Do you want me to put that back on? (*pointing to the blue one which I still had in my hand*)

MB: (*Also whispered.*) No, I should leave it off because, as you said, it's not right is it with that on. So, shall I hide it away? (*Joseph nodded and I put it behind my back.*) Could you tell me anything else about it Leanne?

Leanne: If we join that six one there would be seven. (*pointing to the hat with '6' written on it*)

MB: So if we counted that six as well ...

Joseph: There would be seven.

MB: Yes.

Joseph: So if we took that one off, then there would be six. (*pointing now to the last white one*)

Xanthe: If we take the white one off there would be the right number.

MB: What, if we were counting the top one as well. (*This was said to agree with them, not really as a question.*)

Xanthe: Yes. We do! If you take the white one off. So you can count that one (*pointing to the hat*), and go up to six.

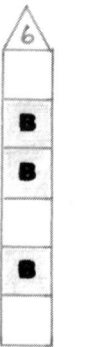

B = Blue

Figure 8.2 I rearranged the stick thus

76

Joseph: No. If you take the white one off and count there, then there would be five ... no ... um ... there is one, two, three, four, five, six. If you take that one off there would be five wouldn't there? (*Joseph was pointing to the last white one. I took it off, giving the result shown in figure 8.3.*)

Xanthe: If you do that one ... if you count this one (*the hat*), there ... there'd be six like this: one, two, three, four, five, six. So I'm right.

MB: And Joseph's right as well, isn't he? There's five if we *don't* count that one and six if we *do* count that one (*pointing to the hat*). If I put that one on there's six if I do count ... er six if I count ... that one ... (*putting the end white one back again*)

Joseph: And if we take the top one off ... Can we take the top one off?

MB: Yes. (*I took the hat off, giving the result shown in figure 8.4.*)

Cirwyn: (*Laughing.*) Uh! Uh! Uh! Uh!

Joseph: There'd still be the right number wouldn't there?

Xanthe: One, two, three, four, five, six.

Cirwyn: (*Laughing.*) Seven?

MB: (*Laughing.*)

Cirwyn: I know what: if you see that number (*looking at the '6' on the hat I had in my hand*), that means there's six of them blocks.

MB: That's what it looks like, doesn't it? Yes, Cirwyn!

Cirwyn: Now there's six.

MB: Now there's six.

Joseph: But if you put that on (*meaning the hat*), there'll be seven. If we take that off there'll be the right number.

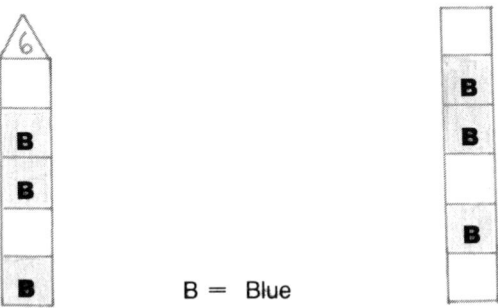

B = Blue

Figure 8.3 The stick after removing one white cube   *Figure 8.4* Taking the hat off

77

Xanthe: But if we don't have that on we won't know which ... how many there is!

MB: (*Laughing.*) No! So there's a problem isn't there? If we have it on there's seven, so that's wrong if we're counting this. If we have it off, then we don't know straight away how many there are!

Xanthe: If we take the white one off and not that one (*meaning the hat*) then we know how many it is. If we ... (*I took the white one off, giving the result shown in figure 8.5.*)

Cirwyn: (*Interrupting.*) Look: five!

Leanne: If we take that one off there would be one, two, three, four, five.

Joseph: And if we took that one off (*pointing to the bottom cube*), there would be ...

Cirwyn: Four! (*I took it off, giving the result shown in figure 8.6.*)

Joseph: And if we took that one off (*pointing to the bottom cube*), there would be ...

Xanthe: Three!

Cirwyn: Three! (*I took it off, giving the result shown in figure 8.7.*)

Joseph: And if we took that one off (*pointing to the bottom cube*), there would be ...

Xanthe: Two!

Cirwyn: Two! (*I took it off, giving the result shown in figure 8.8.*)

Joseph: And if we took that one off (*pointing to the bottom cube*), there would be one! (*I took it off, giving the result shown in figure 8.9.*) And now we need number one to go on there, don't we? (*meaning a '1' hat, presumably*)

MB: (*Laughing.*) Yes! Except we've only got a number six! (*meaning the '6' hat*) (*The six cubes were by now spread in front of us, separately.*)

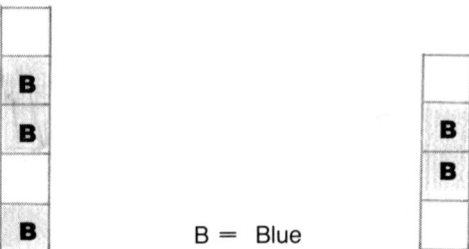

B = Blue

Figure 8.5 I removed the white cube, as suggested by Xanthe

Figure 8.6 Four cubes left

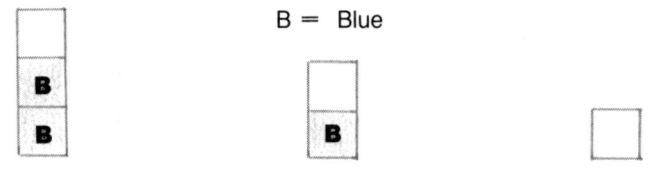

B = Blue

Figure 8.7 Three cubes left   *Figure 8.8* Two cubes left   *Figure 8.9* One cube left

MB:	Could we, perhaps, put these back together again now we've dismantled them?
Leanne:	I can.
MB:	Could you put them together?
Joseph:	I'll put the top one on. (*Leanne arranged them as shown in figure 8.10.*) White, blue, white ... no! ... blue, white ... oh! phew! phew! ... blue, white; blue, white; blue, white.
MB:	Is that the same as we had it before?
Joseph:	One, two, three, four, five, six.
Cirwyn:	No.
Leanne:	No.
Xanthe:	No: we had two next to each other.
Leanne:	That wasn't the same as what we had before.
MB:	How is it different, Leanne?
Leanne:	Because ...
Cirwyn:	My Nanny knitted this! (*pulling at her cardigan*)
MB:	Did she, Cirwyn?
Leanne:	Because ...
Cirwyn:	My Nan knits a lot of things!
Leanne:	... last time there was blue there.
MB:	And this time?
Leanne:	There's white there. (*Meanwhile Joseph was taking Leanne's arrangement to pieces and putting the cubes back as they were originally, as shown in figure 8.11.*)
MB:	And Joseph's remembered what it's like.
Joseph:	(*Counting the cubes.*) One, two, three, four, five, six.
MB:	Well done!
Joseph:	But there was actually that one ... (*inaudible conversation followed this.*)
MB:	Cirwyn, could you Cirwyn, come here and tell us anything else about this?
Cirwyn:	There's three blues and three whites.
MB:	That's something else which Cirwyn's noticed, isn't it? Xanthe, have a look. Cirwyn says that there's

79

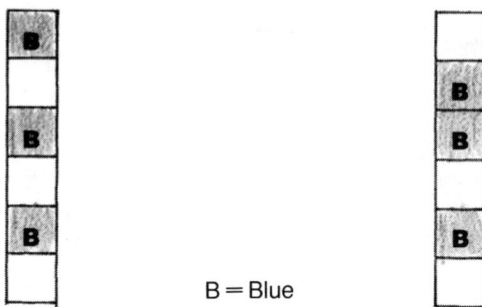

B = Blue

Figure 8.10 Lianne's rearrangement   Figure 8.11 Joseph rearranged the cubes
                                      back to their original order

three blues and three whites.

Joseph: We could change that around a little bit, couldn't we?
           (*Joseph took the cubes and started to rebuild the stick
           again.*)
MB: (*To Xanthe.*) Could you just sit down?
Joseph: There'd still be six but they're changed round a little
           bit aren't they? (*Joseph had put the cubes together as
           shown in figure 8.12.*)
MB: Look what Joseph's done! Yes, you've changed it
           right around, haven't you Joseph! How could you
           talk about what Joseph's done?
Leanne: Three whites joined up and three blues joined up.
Cirwyn: And they're the same colour in the same pile.
MB: The same colour in the same pile. Yes! Would you
           like to do it differently, Cirwyn? (*Cirwyn took the
           cubes and started to make a different stick.*)
Joseph: I thought of a good way, didn't I?
MB: You did.
Xanthe: Next time, I'm going to thought of a good way. [*sic.*]

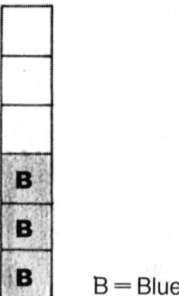

B = Blue

Figure 8.12 Joseph's next rearrangement

80

Part III
ANALYSIS

PRELIMINARY NOTE

To make the best use of the three chapters in part III, you will need to have read at least some of the case-studies in part II. Obviously you will then have acquired some of your own ideas about the nature of the mathematics which featured in the sessions; the children's initiatives; and ways in which I acted. Some of these ideas might be well formed and easy to state; others might be much more tentative, sketchy and hard to express. Whatever your impressions, I shall, of course, be unaware of them and I am conscious that in writing from my own perspective it could seem as if I am ignoring that any alternatives could exist. I want to make it clear at the outset that *I do not wish to impose my thinking as if it comprises the only possible account.* The questions/invitations directed specifically to the reader throughout my analyses should keep serving as a reminder of this. I also want to note that *in no way do I view what I am writing as an exhaustive treatment.* I am fully conscious of making selections, ignoring some themes completely and only scratching the surface of others. In what follows I have picked out and examined some features which strike me in particular and hope that, through resonating with or jarring with your own ideas, these might contribute to the evolution of aspects of your own thinking.

9

THE MATHEMATICS

OVERVIEW

Before analysing any particular part of the mathematics in detail, it may be helpful to try to gain some sort of overview of where the mathematics can be seen in one of the case-studies.

You might find it interesting to choose one of the case-studies and jot down what mathematics you see in it yourself.

For no special reason, I have chosen the 'Christmas trees' case-study (chapter 6) for this purpose. At this stage of my thinking I recognise the following as mathematical elements in the episode:

- Counting/recognising numbers of elements (throughout).
- Counting numbers of elements in subsets, then counting the number of elements in the whole set (e.g. Lucy (5.03) saying she had one red and four blue shapes, then finding that this gave five shapes altogether).
- Counting the number of elements in a set, then thinking of it split into subsets and counting the number of elements in each of those (e.g. Claire (5.02) counting all her shapes on the tree, then counting the squares and circles separately).
- Recognising shapes and naming them (throughout).
- Learning the names of shapes (e.g. Andrew (5.07) learning which shapes to call 'circles' and which to call 'squares').
- Structuring (e.g. Maria (5.02) placing just squares on the spokes of the tree).
- Classifying/sorting (e.g. Louise (5.04) counting her red shapes separately from her blue shapes).
- Deciding what to include/exclude (e.g. Louise including her gingerbread man in her set of red shapes but not in her set of blue shapes).
- Patterning (e.g. Sara (5.02) making a pattern with one red triangle, one blue triangle, etc. along the centre of her tree).
- Thinking ahead (e.g. Sara saying which colour would come next in her pattern of triangles).

- Recognising equivalence (e.g. Sara finding she had the same number of blue triangles as red triangles in her pattern).
- Using/recognising one-to-one correspondence (e.g. Andrew putting one shape on each spoke of his tree).
- Exhausting possibilities (e.g. Andrew making one red circle, one blue circle; one red triangle, one blue triangle; one red square, one blue square).
- Using words like 'a few', 'more', 'lots' (e.g. Daniel (5.06) commenting on there being lots of red crayons and lots of blue crayons).
- Using 'all' and 'some' (e.g. Maria saying that all her squares were blue and all her circles were red).
- Reasoning (e.g. Louise working out that it was a triangle which had fallen on the floor).

How does this relate to what you thought? Is my list different from yours?

How do these mathematical elements connect with the school syllabus printed on pp. 10–11 ... or to the list of processes on p. 3?

It is with questions such as the last two that the rest of this chapter will be concerned.

COVERING THE SYLLABUS

Let us examine some of the case histories in relation to the school's syllabus for number in the reception class.

You might like to have a go at an analysis yourself, using this school's syllabus or your own.

In figure 9.1, the syllabus has been reprinted from pages 10–11. The dots indicate where items from the syllabus occurred in three of the activities. The stars show where the children went beyond the items in some way.

What emerges to be commented on?

Having been completed, the grid now looks as if it is definite, unambiguous and fixed. It reveals nothing of the struggles and dilemmas which accompanied the making of it. Consider a few of the decisions/problems I made/faced when compiling it:

1   In putting on a dot I have drawn no attention to the number of times an item occurred. Trying to do so would have presented all sorts of problems and could have proved misleading:

- I cannot possibly be aware of all instances of the items. Much is likely to be private to the children.

	Circle arrangements (chapter 3)	Six by six squares (chapter 4)	Number squares (chapter 5)	A stick of cubes (chapter 8)
(a) Cardinal number: finding the number of elements in sets.	• *	•	• *	•
(b) For a given number, finding an appropriate set.	•			
(c) Ordinal number: Using and recognising 'first', 'second', 'third' etc.		•		
(d) Using knowledge of the ordering of numbers.			•	•
(e) Learning number names.	*			
(f) Writing and recognising numerals.	• *		• *	•
(g) Comparing numbers of objects; recognising and setting up relationships: more, less, same.	•		•	•
(h) Simple addition.	*		• *	•
(i) Simple groupings.	•	•	•	•
(j) Recognising and finding 'half' of objects.		•		

All based on the numbers 0 to 10

Key: • item occurred during this activity.
  ★ children went beyond the item in this activity.

Figure 9.1 The syllabus

- Just one occurrence of something could be particularly poignant for a child, more so than several occurrences of something else.

2   Similarly, I have not marked out individual participation. When first reflecting on an activity, one might think that just one child was involved in a particular item but more probing might suggest that it is difficult to distinguish who was involved. For example, Jody-Blue (5.01) was the only one to shade in half-squares and use the word 'half' in the six by six squares episode (chapter 4, p. 37) but some of the rest of the group might have heard her comments about in some way themselves.

3   There is no doubt about the appropriateness of inserting a dot in some of the spaces. For example, the group's counting throughout the number squares activity (chapter 5, p. 45) leaves no doubt that a dot is required under (a) 'Cardinal number: Finding the number of elements in sets.' Not everything, however, is so cut and dried. For example, when Ben (5.05) switches a 1 dot to a 2 dot and realises that this means that the total 6 should become 7 (chapter 5, p. 48), is it appropriate merely to classify this as (h) 'Simple addition'?

Do any of these problems connect with your own filling in of class record-sheets or making assessments using the attainment targets from the National Curriculum?

Through involvement in the activities, the children have certainly been covering items from the number syllabus. Indeed, we can make all sorts of informal assessments of their ideas and capabilities. So, for example, in the 'Number squares' activity (chapter 5) we find that Vanessa (5.07) already knows how to write the numerals for 'twelve' (p. 50); that Ben (5.05) can add one to six without having to count again from the beginning (p. 48); and that Anne-Marie (5.08) can use a number-ladder successfully up to seventeen (p. 51). (See the appendix, pp. 172–4, for an analysis in terms of the National Curriculum.)

Moreover, during each session, *several* items featured. When we teach by setting closed and prescriptive tasks we often have just one or two items in mind on which we want the children to concentrate. For example, a worksheet in which the children are required to count sets of objects and write the appropriate numeral against each would involve them in (a) and (f) from figure 9.1 but with little likelihood of anything else.

Have a look at some commercially produced worksheets or workcards (or even your own!) in this context.

Perhaps not setting limits on which items will occur can encourage children to see and forge connections between things which otherwise are in danger of being enclosed in watertight compartments? We can all think of occasions when we have moaned about a child failing to see one idea in relation to another: but perhaps the fault was ours?

Of course, it might be argued that the children are just 'flitting' over the categories listed in the syllabus. The following points seem relevant in this context:

1 Each episode analysed here was just one of many sessions with the children. Items from the syllabus were returned to again and again.
2 Why should we expect efficient learning to take place only when children are concentrating on one or two specific items, chosen by the teacher?
3 As the pupils themselves exerted quite a high degree of control over the activities, it seems likely that whatever has happened is more natural to them in some sense than the situations to which tightly imposed teacher-given tasks might lead.
4 Our models of learning often seem to carry with them the notion that children need to 'fully understand' things before moving on to something else. An alternative view is that children (and the rest of us) learn by revisiting ideas again and again, adding to them and modifying them as they range over different contexts. Instead of thinking in terms of words like:

  smooth
    continuous
      rounded off

when referring to learning, maybe we should concentrate on others such as:

  jagged
    discontinuous
      open-ended.

Add your own!

Linked with point (4) is the fact that when setting closed tasks for children one often finds oneself making decisions about what should come before what else. But this is one's own ordering and hence is not necessarily appropriate to the children who will be carrying out the tasks. We might have thought that a lot of work on, say, (a) and (b) from figure 9.1 should precede work on, say, (g), (h) and (i) but in the analysis of the case-studies we find them all intermingled. To take a more specific example, one might assume that the children's number work should be based on the numbers nought to ten first 'until they are confident with those' (whatever that might mean); then on eleven to thirty, say; then on thirty-one to fifty, say. In the 'Circle arrangements' activity, however, we find Matthew (5.05) breaking out of the bounds of such sequencing. His determination to count all of the spots means that the potential foci for his learning become the names of multiples of ten and the fact that it is not sensible to repeat the same word in a counting sequence (see chapter 3, p. 20).

In several of the case-studies we find the children going beyond what was expected of them in the reception class. To what do the uses of '*' in figure 9.1 refer? Let us consider the * entries for the circle arrangements activity:

Re (a) Matthew (5.05) and Sam (5.03) have shown themselves capable of counting well beyond ten (p. 20).
Re (e) They have also been involved in learning and using number names beyond ten (see p. 20).
Re (f) They have considered how to write, and have also written numerals beyond ten (see p. 21).
Re (h) The instances in which Jemma (5.04) rubs out some of her spots could perhaps be classified as informal *subtraction* (see p. 22).

Through not confining the children to work specified by the syllabus, we have glimpsed abilities which would otherwise most likely have remained hidden. For all the time we ourselves impose limits on tasks, we are in danger of not doing justice to children's potential. How often do children find the tasks we set them trivial and boring?

Sometimes a syllabus can be confining in such a subtle way that we might not even be aware of it. For example, item (a) in figure 9.1 implies the tying of counting to *objects*, yet young children often seem to enjoy counting for counting's sake. The structure of the numeral system has to be learned as well. And where is the scope for children to start gaining a grasp of the idea that numbers go on and on for ever? Young children often seem to take great delight in participating in conversations which hinge on such a notion.

A superficial glance at figure 9.1 might give rise to a comment that the activities described in chapters 4, 5 and 8 are no good for encouraging children to learn number names. Generalisations like this need to be avoided, however. Had the children featured in those chapters been insecure in their use of the number names nought to ten, then this might well have emerged as something to be worked on. As it was, the children seemed familiar with them and hence focusing on this category would have been inappropriate.

Can you suggest other false 'conclusions'?

The richness of some parts of the activities cannot possibly be summed up by simple mention of the items on the syllabus. For example, consider the sequence in chapter 5 where Ben (5.05) learns how to write '12' and then finds out some facts about the representation of other numbers greater than ten (see p. 50).

What other examples illustrate how the grid in figure 9.1 does not reflect the richness of what happened? Are there parallels with your own check lists or the attainment targets from the National Curriculum?

Each of the listed content items could be analysed, opening up more items to be considered, then more items within those. For example, 'Finding the number of elements in sets' could be expanded to 'Finding the number of elements in a set

- by counting;
- by instant recognition;
- using one-to-one correspondence.'

Indeed, an analysis of Lianne's (5.03) comments on her colouring of the six by six squares (pp. 37–9) suggests that she was involved in all three modes within a short space of time.

These sub-categories could themselves then be focused in on further. For example, features of the way in which children *co-ordinate* their counting could be examined in these ways:

- counting by assigning a word to each object;
- counting each object only once;
- stopping the count at the correct place;
- using the conventional string of counting words in the correct order without leaving any out and without repeating any.

And we would want children to recognise that the same number is/should be arrived at:

- if different people do the counting;
- if the objects are counted in a different order;
- if the objects are re-arranged.

And could we subdivide even further? The result could be pages and pages of little categories. Where would it end? And suppose each one of these little categories now becomes the focus of a prescribed task? No wonder we often feel we have 'too much to get through'! I find this paralysing, even counter-productive.

Are we not often trapped like this? What are the alternatives?

I stated at the outset that my investigation would mainly focus on 'number' as a specific area of mathematics. This is why I have only commented upon the school's number syllabus in the foregoing discussion. Before leaving this section, however, it seems important to acknowledge what must already be obvious to the reader: other areas of mathematics have featured in the case studies.

Just because one intends that children will work on a particular type of mathematics, this does not mean that they have to do so in isolation. Just because *we* see some boundaries, this does not mean that young children will do so, nor indeed that it is necessary to make the boundaries explicit. Several areas can often be fruitfully combined.

PROCESSES

We can consider another dimension to the mathematics in the case-studies: how have mathematical 'processes' featured in the sessions?

Figure 1.2 (page 5) displays a range of processes which occur typically in mathematics. If I re-write these in list form and analyse the sessions described in chapters 3, 4, 5 and 8 for evidence of them, then I obtain the grid in figure 9.2.

Similar remarks could be noted about the making of this grid as were noted about the making of the one in figure 9.1 (see points 1, 2 and 3 on pages 86–8). At least three further points seem relevant here too:

4   Writing these processes in list form has necessarily imposed an order on them. The proximity of some processes to others might be useful in suggesting connections between them but the vast complexity of relationships has not been done justice to at all.

The array in figure 1.2 of chapter 1 does not do justice to the complexity either. Could any diagram?

5   Different people might consider some of the processes in different ways. For example, I would tend to reserve 'proving' as a label for reasoning deductively from given axioms, but some people use it in less restricted ways.

6   Some of the processes overlap. For some events I have put a dot against two processes at the same time. For example, the way in which Ilona (5.04) shaded in her sheet of circles (figure 3.4) could be noted both as 'structuring' and as 'patterning'.

The sheer number of processes occurring in each session is striking. This is particularly true of the 'A stick of cubes' activity (chapter 8) when one remembers that this is a transcript of just ten minutes of an activity!

In how many processes might children engage when carrying out tasks such as those on the worksheets on p. 11? What happens in your own experience?

Some of the processes have occurred across all three activities. A few of the processes have not occurred at all. One might ask, therefore, if they are perhaps inappropriate for children of this age? Given the often staggering capabilities shown by children, I am wary of putting any ceiling on my expectations of what children of any particular age can do, except perhaps that 'proving', viewed as I have mentioned above, seems unlikely to be

Figure 9.2 (opposite) Showing the range of processes which occurred in the activities described in chapters 3, 4, 5, and 8

	Circle arrangements (chapter 3)	Six by six squares (chapter 4)	Number squares (chapter 5)	A stick of cubes (chapter 8)
Searching for/finding patterns and relationships		•		
Patterning	•	•	•	•
Conjecturing	•	•	•	
Testing	•			•
Verifying	•			•
Refuting	•			
Abstracting	•	•		•
Generalising	•			
Modifying			•	
Proving				
Exhausting a situation	•	•		
Reasoning	•	•	•	•
Justifying				•
Explaining	•	•	•	•
Demonstrating				
Interpreting	•	•	•	•
Extrapolating				
Interpolating				
Checking	•	•	•	•
Symbolising	•		•	
Manipulating				
Representing	•		•	
Recording	•	•	•	
Visualising	•			•
Conceptualising	•	•	•	•
Seeking consistency	•			•
Deciding on rules	•	•		
Using rules	•	•		
Defining	•	•	•	
Deciding on/recognising equivalences	•	•	•	•
Deciding on/recognising differences	•	•	•	•
Searching for solutions		•		
Using solutions to help find others	•	•	•	
Modelling				
Designing algorithms and procedures				
Seeking more efficient methods				
Transforming	•		•	•
Including	•	•		•
Excluding	•	•		•
Classifying	•	•	•	•
Quantifying	•	•	•	•
Calculating				
Counting	•	•	•	•
Putting a measure on	?			
Measuring				
Estimating		•		
Structuring	•	•	•	•
Systematising	•			
Ordering		•	•	•
Comparing	•	•	•	•

93

appropriate for 4 and 5 year olds! Furthermore, there was nothing special about my choice of the case-studies for analysis in figure 9.2: I certainly did not choose them because I thought they encompassed all possible processes which are likely to arise. Examples of other processes might well occur in other sessions. Indeed, in the 'Plates of biscuits' activity (chapter 7) we find the children *extrapolating* from data, continuing patterns they have established on their number ladders.

Let me state something here which I am in danger of not drawing attention to because it has become so obvious to me whilst analysing the case-studies. In answer to the question posed on p. 3, we have certainly seen that *children as young as 4 and 5 can become involved in the processes listed, within mathematics*. We cannot think of such processes as 'too sophisticated', relevant only to older children. We see the young infants described participating in them quite naturally.

Now we might ask whether these processes differ in kind when we talk of older children or mathematicians themselves engaging in them? Let us consider a specific process and see what light can be shed on such a general question.

In figure 9.1 I have noted that symbolising occurs in the 'Circle arrangements' activity (chapter 3) and in the 'Number squares' activity (chapter 5). What form does it take? Each time children say something we could talk of 'symbolising' since to use words is to use symbols. However, I had something much more specific in mind: the children are using numerals to record numbers and, incidentally, learning points about how to do so. This is so obvious that we might easily overlook it.

So here we find children using conventional symbols in the course of their activities. This is, of course, typical of what we expect older children, and mathematicians, to be doing too, though one obvious difference is that older children (and mathematicians!) would be familiar with many more conventional symbols than these young children are. But this is not a difference in the *kind* of activity.

What of other facets to symbolising? When working at mathematics myself I sometimes need to make up a sign to designate something. In the case-studies examined so far there have not been examples of this but consider these:

On a slightly later occasion than the 'A stick of cubes' activity, Joseph (4.11) and Cirwyn (5.01) were putting together strips of four squares and

Figure 9.3 Joseph and Cirwyn's arrangement of cubes

Figure 9.4 Joseph's code

strips of five squares (see figure 9.3) to see which other length strips they could make. After a while they found it difficult to remember all of the lengths they had made so far and Joseph came up with the idea of marking them off on a number ladder like the one seen in figure 7.4. He said he would tick the numbers he could make and Cirwyn said she would put circles by hers. Then Joseph added that he would put circles by the ones he could *not* make but Cirwyn said she would leave these blank. After a while, Joseph discovered that some of the numbers against which he had put circles *could* be made after all. He put ticks over the circles for those. Later, when he was satisfied that some of the other numbers marked with circles definitely could not be made, he decided to put a line through the circles to symbolise that. He ended up with signs like that in figure 9.4.

In his book *Children and number* (1986), Martin Hughes gives examples of children aged from 3.01 to 5.10 playing a game in which they made up their own symbols to represent three, two, one and no bricks.

John (3.06) was playing with a cardboard box. At one point his mother found him looking at it and repeating 'One, two, three, four; one, two, three, four; ...'. She asked him where he could see that. He showed her '1 4 3 0' which was written on the box and said, 'One', pointing to the '1'; '*Pretend that's a two*', pointing to the '0'; 'Three', pointing to the '3'; and 'Four', pointing to the '4'. He knew that '0' was not the usual symbol for two but was happy to think about it as such.

So here we glimpse examples of children of reception age, and much younger, actually making some sort of a decision about how to symbolise something.

The above discussions about a specific process would suggest, therefore, that at least some of the processes do not differ in kind from the processes engaged in by older children/mathematicians. Rather it is what they range over which might differ.

Which other processes might not differ in kind? Which processes might differ?

95

Some more parallels:

Deciding on rules

Joanne, an 11 year old, is seeing how many decominoes she can make with pairs of congruent pentominoes. She decides to investigate only those decominoes with holes in them, for example:

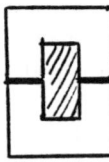

Figure 9.5 An example of Joanna's decomino patterns

She also states 'We are not allowing the shapes to be joined at corners, only at sides.' She says that:

Figure 9.6 An unacceptable pattern

would not be acceptable.[1]

Jemma (5.04) allows this sort of arrangement:

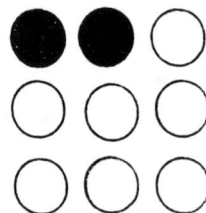

Figure 9.7 Jemma's arrangements

but not this sort:

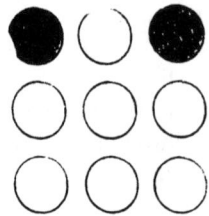

Figure 9.8 Jemma would not allow this pattern

when colouring two spots from each of the sets of nine spots on her sheet (p. 23). She stipulates that the spots must be side by side.

Seeking consistency

In giving a lecture in 1900 about what he saw as the schedule for research in the twentieth century, the mathematician David Hilbert listed proving the consistency of the axioms of arithmetic as one of the main problems to be tackled. He himself spent a great deal of time working on this and other consistency problems.[2]

Much of the first part of the 'A stick of cubes' activity (chapter 8) consists of the children grappling with the inconsistency of being faced with seven unifix cubes but with the numeral '6' attached to the stick. Their various suggestions are concerned with making it right. For example, Xanthe (4.10) says, 'Seven. You've got to take one off ... The blue one. Then there'd be the right number' (p. 75).

Transforming

Every time we alter an expression to make it more amenable to further treatment we are involved in transforming. For example in

$$\begin{array}{r} 64 \\ -27 \end{array}$$

the sixty-four (sixty and four) can become fifty and fourteen in order to give us sufficient units in the right-hand column from which to subtract seven.

When shading in his sheet of sets of nine spots in the 'Circle arrangements' activity, Matthew (5.05) attends to trying to find different arrangements of *eight* spots initially, but then transforms the problem into focusing on different places for the *one* spot left each time (p. 24).

Reasoning

Every time one is engaged in something more than the mechanical carrying out of a calculation or other process etc., one is likely to be involved in some sort of reasoning. Consider, for example, the great amount of reasoning involved in Euclid's proof that there is no greatest prime:

Suppose P is the greatest prime. But consider multiplying together all the primes up to P and adding 1 to the result. This new number, X say, cannot be divisible by any of the primes up to P since it would give 1 as remainder on division by any one of them. Hence either X is prime or it is divisible by a prime between P and X. In either case there is a prime greater than P.

The case-studies described in chapters 3 to 8 are peppered with examples of children reasoning. To reconsider just one of many examples here, think of Ben's (5.05) sensible reasoning in the 'Number squares' activity (p. 50) when claiming that twelve would not be written as '12'. ('Twelve? That doesn't look like a twelve! A twelve is more than a one and a two, I bet it is!')

Classifying

A group of 10 and 11 year olds classified some prime numbers as ones which were the sums of squares (for example, $13 = 4 + 9$) and ones which could not be built up as such (for example, 11), trying to find rules for ascribing the numbers to both sets.[3] This is a classic problem, first worked on centuries ago.

Whilst completing her Christmas tree, Louise (5.04) announced 'I've got five blues and seven reds.' She has classified her decorations as blue or red. Others classified theirs according to the different shapes (p. 54).

Other examples?

So far, symbolising has been the only process to be examined in any depth. We could, of course, probe into the nature of all the other processes too. To try to do justice to their complexity, however, would take a great deal of space. Instead of attempting such a vast undertaking I will concentrate on opening up points about just two further processes: conjecturing and structuring. I have chosen these because there are some issues associated with them which seem particularly significant to a discussion about 4 and 5 year olds.

Conjecturing

Often when engaged in mathematics myself I find that I become involved in a sequence of processes which could be described as searching for patterns or relationships; making conjectures as to how these patterns/relationships will continue; testing to see if they do; then either generalising about what seems will always happen and going on to try to prove it or reason why it should be so; or, having found that my original conjecture was not borne out in practice, modifying it and testing anew.

A simple example

I want to try to establish a rule to establish which primes are the sums of two squares and which are not. (This links with the example under 'classifying' p. 97.)

I find that these primes are the sums of two squares:

2	5	13	17	29	37	41	53
1+1	1+4	4+9	1+16	4+25	1+36	16+25	4+49

(whereas the ones between them are not). I take differences between them in the hopes of finding a pattern:

2		5		13		17		29		37		41		53
	3		8		4		12		8		4		12	

and notice that, after 3, the differences go 8, 4, 12; 8, 4, 12. I am happy to ignore the difference of 3 temporarily because it comes from the presence of the 2 and there is something strange about 2; it is the only *even* prime. I wonder if the differences will continue 8, 4, 12; 8, 4, 12; 8, 4, 12 ... This should mean that the next prime number to be the sum of two squares is 61. I test this conjecture and find it to be correct since $61 = 25 + 36$ and no other numbers between 53 and 61 are both primes *and* the sum of two squares. The next one should be 65. Oh! My theory falls down straight away because 65 is not prime. I shall need to think about the examples again ...

'Conjecturing' here, then, is part of a web of processes. Is there any evidence of conjecturing featuring like this in the case-studies of the 4 and 5 year olds? Engagement in such a web has become what I might describe as an 'automatic' procedure for me, but one might imagine that it is too sophisticated for 4 and 5 year olds.

But let us consider the 'Plates of biscuits' activity (chapter 7). We could analyse part of this as follows:

- The children saw a pattern in their sets of answers when these were marked on a number ladder.
- They continued the pattern beyond their original answers.
- They guessed how some of these new numbers could be obtained using their original structurings.
- They tested to see if their guesses were correct.

Is not this guessing and testing of guesses closely akin to the making and testing of conjectures embedded in the web of processes considered above? I say 'closely akin to' rather than 'the same as' for a reason. I talked of my 'making conjectures as to how these patterns/relationships will continue' but I said of the children that they 'continued the pattern' and 'guessed how some of these new numbers could be obtained'. I feel that there is a subtle difference but it is difficult to pinpoint. Referring to the primes example might help:

My first conjecture in this example is that there will continue to be differences of 8, 4, 12 between the numbers which are both primes and sums of squares. I do not blindly continue the 8, 4, 12 pattern: I *do it with a purpose in mind.* I hope that it will still serve to pinpoint numbers with the properties I am seeking.

The children, however, might well have continued their patterns blindly, not being conscious at that time that it would be reasonable to guess that their newly marked numbers might be the next answers in their plates of biscuits work. For them, 'continuing the pattern' and 'guessing how these new numbers could be obtained' are not necessarily fused together in the same way as they are for me. Indeed, *I* ask them 'Where would it go next, do you think, if we were to put another dot on?' (p. 67) and this could be taken to refer just to the pattern itself, *in vacuo.* When the children do continue the pattern, my remark 'That's a guess, isn't it, at where those numbers will go?' *connects for me, but not necessarily for the children,* the patterning back with the biscuits work.

Nevertheless, the potential for the children to make the connection is there. And, after all, the children subsequently became involved in guessing how the new numbers could be obtained using the structuring already put into the biscuits work. Perhaps in this episode we see some fundamental groundwork being laid for the intertwining of conjecturing and patterning – patterning with a purpose – at a later data.

Linked with this last point is the fact that one of the fundamental differences between children's guesses and our guesses is that ours are more likely to be better informed. We have a much wider world-view, background knowledge, perception of appropriate kinds of explanation, causation, generative formulae, etc. Children can certainly conjecture, but they need to become aware of and practice the web of associated refining processes which often come automatically to those with more experience.

What about other examples of conjecturing from the case-studies?

From the 'Christmas trees' activity: When I put out the sets of shapes for the children to use as decorations for their trees the children called out 'Circles', then 'Triangles' and Claire (5.02) then said 'The next ones are squares I bet!' (p. 53).

From the 'Number squares' activity: Having looked on a number ladder at some numerals he had never seen before, Ben (5.05) guessed how the next few numbers would be written (p. 50).

From the 'Circle arrangements' activity: In trying to decide whether 'There are nine sets of two dots' was a sensible interpretation of what Jemma had written about her arrangement of her papers, Matthew (5.05) said 'I think there might be' when thinking whether there were nine sets (p. 29).

From the 'Six by six squares' activity: Hayley (4.10) coloured her first six by six square using a pattern of *one* column of each of three colours. She coloured her second six by six square using a pattern of *two* columns of each of the three colours. When thinking how to continue this sequence and deciding to use three columns of each colour, she mentioned only two colours instead of all three, perhaps suggesting some feeling for how many of such blocks could fit on the paper (p. 34).

Do you have any of your own examples of young children making conjectures within a mathematical context?

In each of those examples (and in guessing which numbers would add to give particular ones in the 'Plates of biscuits' activity) we find the children thinking ahead, making some sort of prediction. These predictions are based on considering, albeit briefly/automatically, some elements of situations as they find them at that moment. The children cannot be sure that what they are alluding to will be the case. Indeed, it is this element of uncertainty which turns 'thinking ahead' into 'conjecturing'.

Margaret Donaldson has demonstrated that young children find 'embedded' thinking easier than 'disembedded' thinking. That is, they show the greatest degree of control over situations which arise within a 'context of fairly immediate goals and intentions and familiar patterns of events' (1984, p. 76) and hence which make 'human sense'. Mathematics as it is often encountered in school, however, can seem to children to be disembedded. A statement such as 'Three and five makes eight' could be taught to children without them having had sufficient experience to make such a generalisation from particular instances themselves and to make an abstraction, that is to give the generality a life of its own. Some teachers seek to avoid such disembedded learning by *confining* young children's mathematics to working only with actual objects but this does not face the question of how then, eventually, the children will be able to cope with much greater generalisation/abstraction. Rather, whilst involving young children in meaningful situations we need to find ways of starting to enable them to lift their thinking above the immediate context, prizing it out of its original matrix, going beyond the here and now.

Is this not exactly what is starting to happen when children are making conjectures as in the examples above?

> Ben's (5.05) thinking about the continuation of numerals beyond 22 seems worthy of a particular remark here. He is operating within what we might term a 'formal system': the objects about which he is thinking are mere marks on the paper (p. 50)

In many other instances in the case-studies we can see the children not necessarily 'conjecturing' as such, but definitely thinking ahead. For example, the 'A stick of cubes' activity (chapter 8) is absolutely full of 'If . . .' statements:

> Leanne (5.00): If we join that six one there would be seven. (p. 76)
> Joseph (4.10): So if we took that one off there would be six. (p. 76)
> Xanthe (4.10): If we take the white one off there would be the right number. (p. 76) etc.

Every time a child thinks ahead she is starting to push her thinking beyond the immediate. Sometimes this 'thinking ahead' expresses young children's awakening awareness of there being no limit to same processes (cf. p. 90 here too). Consider the following example.

Matthew (5.04), Ben (5.05) and Rachel (5.01) had been working with little cards on which were stuck either one, two, three or four coloured spots. They had then stuck some spots on blank cards themselves. At the end of the session Ben suddenly had the idea that they could put different numbers of spots on other cards another time. This conversation followed:

> Matthew: We haven't done a six.
> Ben: We could do a seven.
> Matthew: We can do any number.
> Ben: Not a hundred!
> Rachel: Anything we like!
> Matthew: If we had lots . . .

Ben:	Not a *hundred* you can't.
Matthew:	Oh yes we can!
Ben:	We can't on just a little piece of paper.
Matthew:	Yes we can.
Ben:	No we can't! How can we do that?
Matthew:	Can: get a bigger piece! 'Cos I've got a paper that's about *that* big. (*holding his hands far apart*)
Ben:	If we had our little pieces of paper and joined them all together and then we could do that.
Matthew:	We could make a big one.
Ben:	We could make fifty-nine hun ... thousand!
MB:	Good gracious, that would be a big number!
Ben:	Yes. Then we could go all over the world! (*This was followed by peels of laughter!*)
Matthew:	No they won't ...
Ben:	Yes they will!
Matthew:	They'll go across to another world!
Ben:	Yeah ... they'll go over the sea and we could ... we could go over ...
Matthew:	We could go over to see Africa! (*More laughter!*)
Ben:	It would go past that! (*Unfortunately, the children were interrupted at this point.*)

Here we find 5 year olds going way beyond their original arithmetic-of-spots, starting to grapple with ideas of infinity, breaking beyond what can be done in practice, beginning to create a world of untied-down ideas.

Do you have any of your own examples of children using their imagination to go beyond the immediate and particular to generate mathematical ideas?

Structuring

When I first worked with 4 or 5 year olds, the vast amount of structuring which they put into their activities was one of the things which surprised me most. The following point to a few of the many examples of structuring in the case-studies:

From the 'Circle arrangements' activity: In completing her sheet (figure 3.4), Ilona (5.04) has not just shaded in six spots of each set haphazardly, but has decided to:

- make an arrangement and then repeat it across one row;
- make a different arrangement and then repeat that across the middle row; and
- make a different arrangement again and repeat that across the bottom row.

Consider what structuring went into the shading of the other children's sheets.

From the 'Number squares' activity: Having been given the nine jumbled-up little pieces of card, Anne-Marie (5.08) immediately set about sorting them according to the number of dots on each and arranged them in a square (p. 45).

Consider what structuring went into producing the arrangements shown as figures 5.4 to 5.9.

From the 'Christmas trees' activity: Louise (5.04) chose to put one of each of the three different shapes along both sides of her tree (figure 6.1).

Consider what structuring went into the decorating of the other children's Christmas trees.

Moreover, as the time progressed I became aware of a particular facet to some of the structuring which excited me even more. This can best be explained through an example.

In the 'Six by six squares' activity we find Hayley (4.10) producing what is now shown diagrammatically as figure 9.9. (And see figures 4.5, 4.6 and 4.7.)[4]

Not only has she structured her original square, she has continued in a way which might be described as 'playing with the structure'. It is as if (A) has served to define the structure and then in (B) and (C) she has gone on to work with the elements in it – columns of squares – using number in doing so.

Of course, at the start of colouring (A) she might not actually have *intended* to come up with what she did. For example, she might have coloured:

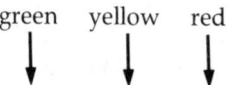

green   yellow   red

with no thoughts other than altering the pencils as she did it and then more or less mechanically repeating the sequence when she ran out of colours. But whatever her original intentions, or lack of them, she was certainly aware of the structure when she had completed the square, for this was

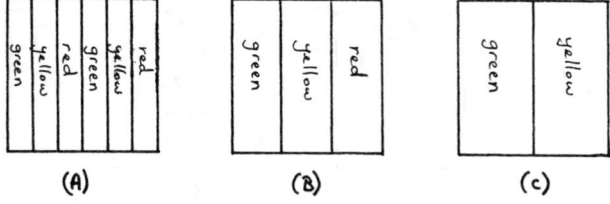

(A)   (B)   (C)

Figure 9.9 Diagrammatic representation of Hayley's work in the earlier activity

apparent from the rhythmic way in which she said, 'I've done green, yellow, red; green, yellow, red' (p. 34).

From that point she certainly operated far from randomly. As we have seen, instead of doing one green, one red and one yellow of her columns of six squares she did two of each, but not necessarily imposing the same order on them: I may have read that into what she had done (see p. 34). Then she did three of each as far as they would fit. Perhaps she did not attempt a fourth example still following the sequence because she perceived in advance it would not be possible?

We can see a similar process at work when she later completed what is now shown diagrammatically as figure 9.10 (and see figure 4.15). Again the first example has defined the structure, then she has operated on it. What does the 'operating on it' consist of here? We do not know how Hayley perceived this but *we* might talk of permuting the elements, changing the order of the elements, adding to an equivalence class, etc.

There is also potential here for trying to exhaust the situation: how many structures like this are there altogether? When Hayley was first producing the squares I do not know if any sense of trying-to-exhaust-the-situation came into her thinking. She could have been focusing on doing 'more' without thinking of doing 'all'. Interestingly enough, though, the following week Alan (4.11) did exhaust the patterns and seemed to feel he could not find any others, though I suspect his reasons behind this were more of the I've-been-looking-for-a-long-time-and-I-can't-find-any-more sort than centring on some awareness that it would actually be *impossible* to find any more.[5] Perhaps, at the very least, the activity has sown some seeds for the children to grasp that there is a limit to the production of some sets?

Is it only Hayley who, of her own volition, has pursued 'structuring' so far as to produce not only an original structure but also to continue to operate within it in some way? No! Far from it! In working with the children over the last two years I have become aware of many such examples. Indeed, a few more of these are evident from some of the other case-studies included in part II. As examples:

In the 'Circle arrangements' activity Sam (5.03) shaded in the circles as shown in figure 9.11 as his second configuration of five spots. He then used this three-

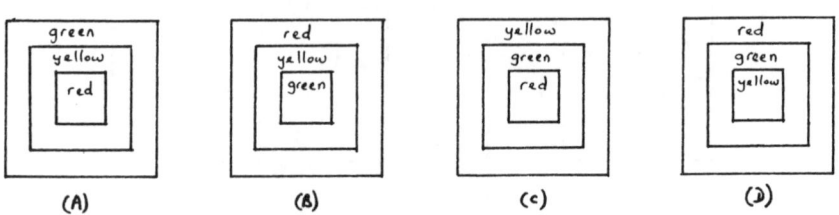

Figure 9.10 Diagrammatic representation of Hayley's later work

104

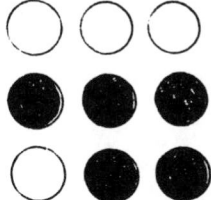

Figure 9.11 Sam's pattern of five spots

and-two structure for the rest of his configurations on the sheet, but operating on it in the sense of moving it round in different orientations (see figure 3.8). *In the 'Plates of biscuits' activity* Ilona (5.04) put one 'biscuit' on to both 'plates' in her first example. She then continued with this structure of using-the-same-number for the rest of the pairs of plates, working through the number sequence from one to four in doing so (see figure 7.2).

Do you have any of your own examples of young children structuring?

One of the points which I have found particularly exciting about this structuring is that there are close parallels with what happens when I am doing mathematics. In short, I continually find myself creating structures and then working on them. But this sounds rather pretentious, is vague and perhaps has an 'ivory tower' feel to it! An example might help to bring out more of what I mean, but readers may ignore it if they wish:[6]

It is usual to represent functions such as y = 2x, y = x + 1, etc. on ordinary graphs, for example:

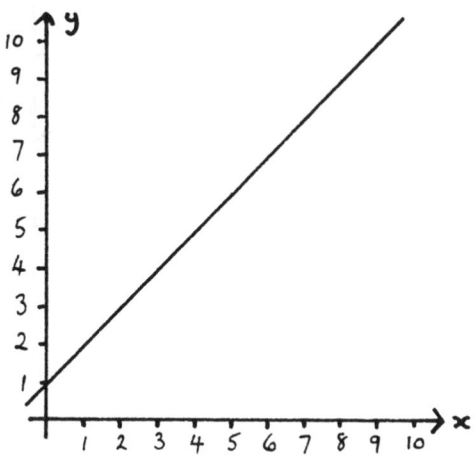

Figure 9.12 y = x + 1

105

but I asked myself, what if we consider a function in modular arithmetic, say y = 2x + 4 modulo 5? I plotted a few graphs, for example:

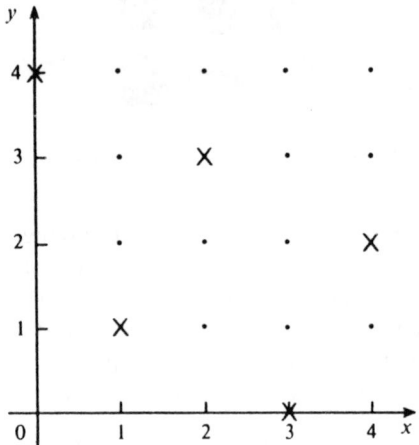

Figure 9.13 y = 2x + 4 (mod. 5)

but felt dissatisfied. They were just collections of points and did not show the cyclic nature of modular arithmetic. I decided to try representing the function through a different form of graph: an arrow diagram. y = 2x + 4 modulo 5 now looked like this:

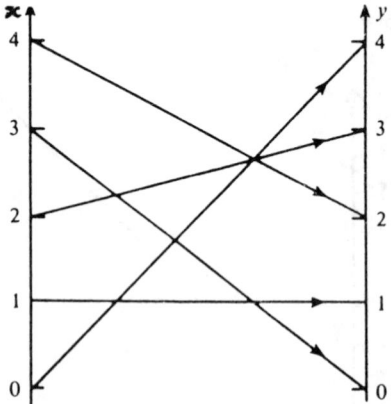

Figure 9.14 y = 2x + 4 (mod. 5)

Somehow this looked more interesting! But the fact that 4 is next to 0 in modulus 5 (stepping on 1 from 4 brings us back to 0 again) was still obscured. I then hit upon the idea of bending round the x and y axes to form concentric circles since then the cyclic nature of modular arithmetic would be more implicit in the diagram. This gave me:

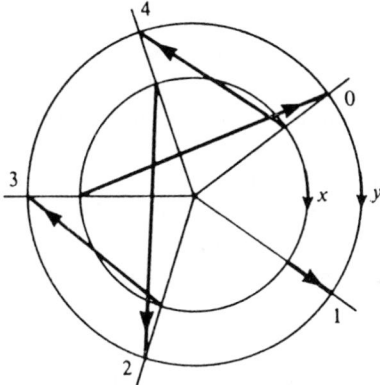

Figure 9.15 y = 2x + 4 (mod. 5)

More interesting still! I tried out the representation of more functions in this way and found, amongst other things, that all the functions I drew of the form y = mx + c modulo n had a line of symmetry. I set about investigating where this line of symmetry occurred; spotted an apparent relationship; made and tested conjectures about its occurrence in other examples; made a generalisation and set about proving it (and, in the course of this, had to modify my original idea that the n in modulo n could be any natural number).

Deciding on the circular arrow diagrams is an example of what I mean by 'creating a structure'. Then I worked within that structure: it had become an object to be explored.

But I am not a professional mathematician. Can I find any support for these views from those who are? Comments from Philip Davis and Reuben Hersh are particularly illuminating here. Davis and Hersh are two established mathematicians whose book *The mathematical experience* (1981) describes what doing mathematics feels like to them. In an intriguing chapter entitled 'True facts about imaginary objects' they write of two facts which they have learnt from their work on mathematics:

Fact 1: Mathematics is our creation; it is about ideas in our minds.
Fact 2: Mathematics is an objective reality in the sense that mathematical objects have definite properties, which we may or may not be able to discover.

(Davis and Hersh 1981, pp. 408–9)

and they go on to claim that 'As mathematicians, we know that we invent ideal objects and then try to discover the facts about them.'

107

This certainly lends support to the creation-of-structures-then-working-within-them idea. Much more could be discussed here, for example, how does this link with the various well-established philosophies concerning the nature of mathematics? How, for example, does the creation of structures link with the 'real world'? But issues such as these are highly complex and would need a great deal of space devoted to them to do them justice. The interested reader would I am sure enjoy consulting Davis and Hersh (1981).

In concluding this section it seems important to make it clear that I am *not* claiming that what the children are doing above is mathematics in any final or polished sense, but it seems fair to view it as mathematics-in-the making at the very least. If we recognise such embryonic mathematics in our classrooms, perhaps we can turn our thoughts to questioning how we can facilitate its growth.

SOME CONNECTIONS

So far, our discussions in this chapter have either been centred on the syllabus or on processes. How do the two connect?

What is listed as the syllabus is what people often term 'content' and we often hear content and processes talked about as if they were somehow unrelated. An immediate counter to such supposed disjointedness is that some items appear under both. 'Comparing' features as a process, but 'Comparing numbers of objects' also appears in the content list; 'Counting' features as a process but 'Finding the number of elements in sets' also appears in the content list (see figures 9.1 and 9.2).

Other overlaps?

Actually, we should not really be at all surprised that this is the case. 'Content' is frequently associated with a view of mathematics as a body of knowledge which consists of certain skills and concepts to be learnt. 'Processes', on the other hand, are frequently associated with a view of mathematics as an activity. But we must remember that what today has acquired the status of 'content' was brought about yesterday through activity. As Brian Griffiths so lucidly writes, 'Over the course of time, some fabricated mathematics eventually becomes modified into a fairly permanent form. Its very permanence leads to it being highly prized, so that when many people refer to 'mathematics', they have in mind only this content, or the fabricated mathematics, and they forget or discount the activity that led to it.' (1983, p. 298)

An example would seem helpful here.

A group of 4 and 5 year olds had spent a session colouring-in strips of squares of different lengths such as those in figure 9.16, using red and green pencils alternately. They had become interested in which numbers of squares gave two red ends, two green ends, or one red and one green end. When I brought in the strips the following session for the group to continue working with them, I commented on them being in a muddle in the envelope and invited Xanthe (4.09) and Leanne (5.00) to sort them out in some way. Leanne started to collect the strips with two red ends saying, 'All the reds on this pile.' Xanthe added 'And all the greens on this end are coming over here' and started to collect the strips with two green ends. After a while I noticed that Leanne had included in her pile a strip with one red end and one green end. I asked Xanthe what *she* thought about that and she claimed that it should be in *her* pile. Then suddenly she had another idea. She turned the strip round and placed it so that the red end went on Leanne's pile and the green end went on her own pile. With an air of satisfaction she announced 'Half goes on each end!'

Here we see children engaged actively and meaningfully in classifying and sorting. When I recounted this episode to a group of teachers, however, one remarked 'They're nearly doing 'sets' aren't they?' Oh! More probing revealed that, to this teacher, 'doing sets' had become inextricably linked with the use of Venn diagrams, putting objects into hoops etc. The processes of classifying and sorting had become ossified into a piece of content called 'sets' in the teacher's mind: an example of what Freudenthal (1983) aptly terms 'false concretisations' (p. 39). Unfortunately, such ossification can lead to topics being presented with little more underlying purpose being suggested than it-must-be-covered-because-it-is-on-the-syllabus. If we want children to see a purpose to what they are doing in mathematics, surely we must strive to avoid such ossification?

Do you know of other examples of 'false concretisations'?

There is also another dimension to the connections between processes and content. Processes do not occur in a vacuum, rather they range over what might be thought of as 'subject matter' in any case. As examples:

1   When Ben (5.05) guessed how the next few numbers following 20, 21 and 22 would be written (p. 50), we could talk of him 'making a conjecture' but it was a conjecture *concerned with number*, or the symbolisation of number to be more precise.

2   When Sam (5.03) said about his two configurations (see figure 9.17)

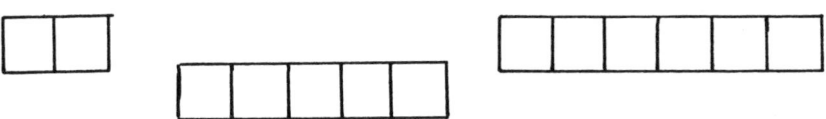

Figure 9.16 Different lengths of squares to be coloured by the children

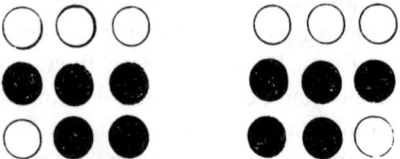

Figure 9.17 Sam's patterns

that 'That one's facing that way and that one's facing that way' (p. 23) we could talk of him 'recognising a difference' but it is a difference in terms of *position in space*. The arrangements are reflections of one another.

Indeed, perhaps one might claim that it is the fact that the processes discussed above range over what we recognise as mathematical subject matter which means that we are looking at mathematics rather than anything else? For consider, in contrast, such remarks as 'If you press harder perhaps you could make that orange pencil come out red' (!) and 'That green's a different shade from this.' Here the making of a conjecture and the recognition of a difference do *not* seem to be concerned with mathematical subject matter. Similar remarks could be made about the snippets of conversation on pp. 3–6.

A qualification seems pertinent here, however. Granted that when processes range over areas such as number or space etc. they are certainly interwoven in mathematics, but perhaps mathematics does not arise *only* in such cases? Much depends on how wide a view one has of the subject in the first place. For example, in *Notes on Mathematics in Primary Schools* (1967) the Association of Teachers of Mathematics claim that 'Mathematics is not just about number and space; it can be said to happen whenever the mind classifies and creates structures' (p. 2). So, whether one is classifying, say, different sorts of angles or different sorts of pencils, both could count as mathematics. Such a definition would allow in cases such as those described under 'structuring' on p. 102 regardless of whether aspects of number or space were significant features in the creation of the structures.

Do we need to restrict 'classifying' or 'creating structures' in any way before counting them as fundamental mathematical processes?

Which other processes could be considered as fundamental to mathematics?

10

THE CHILDREN'S INITIATIVES

The whole of this book is concerned with children taking their own initiative within mathematics. Actually being actively involved in mathematical activity, rather than merely being the passive recipient of already worked-out mathematical facts, necessarily involves one taking initiatives. Since the mathematics discussed in the previous chapter was largely that of mathematical activity, the points in this chapter are inextricably linked to what has been said before. I have separated the analysis into two parts for ease of reference only.

I have referred to the 'children's initiatives' several times already in this book and I hope it has served to convey something of what I conceive as one of the main features of my periods spent with the children. I am not, however, entirely happy with this phrase but can find no simple alternative.

What does 'taking initiatives' imply to you? Do you think this squares with some of the children's actions in the case-studies?

What I want to discuss here, then, is a complex notion which is hard to pin down and label. Perhaps it is best to start trying to communicate what I mean by creating a further impression rather than by immediately plunging into an analysis? With that in mind, please compare the following.

SITUATION (A)

This is an extract from the dialogue given in chapter 8.

I had joined four blue and three white unifix cubes together (as in figure 10.1), but put a '6' hat on the stick instead of a '7'.

(I held the stick up in front of the children.)

MB:	I'd like you to have a look at this. (*Something inaudible was said, then:*)
Cirwyn, Joseph, Xanthe, Leanne:	Six, Six, Six, Six, Six. (*each calling out 'Six' [somebody twice!], presumably looking at the number on the hat*)

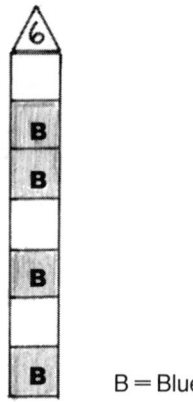

B = Blue

Figure 10.1 The stick of cubes

Joseph: Is there six blocks? (*Pause.*)

MB: Would you like to see, Joseph? (*I handed Joseph the stick.*)

Joseph: One, two, three, four, five, six, *seven*? (*putting his finger on each cube as he counted*) There's more than six, isn't there?

Xanthe: Seven, You've got to take one off.

MB: We've got to take one off, have we?

Xanthe: The blue one. Then there'd be the right number: six.

MB: Would you like to take that off, then, Joseph: the blue one that Xanthe's talking about?

Xanthe: Then there'd be six. (*Joseph took the last blue cube off the stick.*)

Joseph: One, two, three, four, five, six. She's quite right. So there is *six*.

MB: So it was wrong before?

Xanthe: Yes ... to start off with.

*　　　*　　　*

SITUATION (B)

This is a fictitious account, constructed for the purposes of this analysis.

The teacher held up a stick of unifix cubes as in figure 10.1.

Teacher: What does the hat say on top of these cubes?

Children: Six.

Teacher: Right. Now let's count the cubes. (*The teacher pointed to each cube in turn as they were counted.*)

112

Teacher and children together:	One, two, three, four, five, six, seven.
Teacher:	So is that the right hat to go with the cubes?
Children:	No.
Teacher:	Which hat should be on the stick?
Child:	The seven one.
Teacher:	(*To a particular child*) Come and find a seven one then, please, and put it on the stick. (*The child did so.*)
Teacher:	Is that correct now?
Children:	Yes.

Analysis

Let us try to focus on what it is which makes situation (B) different from (A).

In (B) the children's replies and actions are constrained: there is only one correct way of responding to the teacher's questions and instructions in each case. The teacher steers what happens tightly: she controls the course of the sequence entirely.

In (A) there are constraints: the children are required to look at the stick of cubes etc. But there is much more freedom *within* these constraints. Several outcomes are possible. The children themselves participate in steering what happens.

It is this 'participating in what happens' which I have so far referred to as the 'children's initiatives'. Although the idea of taking initiatives captures the essence of what I want to say, somehow it is too 'grand' to describe all the little incidents which link together to constitute an episode such as (A). However, having mentioned my unease with the term, I shall continue to use it occasionally for convenience.

Do any alternative expressions seem reasonable to you?

Let us try to lay bare and tease out further aspects of the notion of steering what happens/taking initiatives.

In (A), indeed in the whole of the 'A stick of cubes' case-study (chapter 8), we find a number of what I call 'moves' by the children which help to determine what happens next. For each move that is made, another would have been conceivable. So, when Xanthe said, 'Seven. You've got to take one off', she might have said something like, 'Seven. You've got to change the hat.' And when Joseph questioned, 'Is there six blocks?' he and the others might never have thought to have questioned this but, say, set about making sticks for themselves with six cubes in them.

Does this mean that we can talk of the children choosing or deciding on what to say/do? There are some dangers here. To talk of someone 'choosing' or 'deciding' may well imply that he is aware of alternatives: he makes a choice between something and something else. But often, even if the teacher can see possibilities for a variety of actions, the children themselves might not be aware of alternatives. I doubt that Xanthe or Joseph consciously weighed up what to say when they made the moves highlighted above. So does it still make sense to talk of the children having 'freedom' to respond? Yes if we think in terms of the children having the freedom to formulate and express their own perceptions. Even if a child has not chosen what to say or do it is still his own way of looking at something which is being given an opportunity to come to the fore. It can be helpful to think in terms of freedom *from* something rather than freedom *to do* something and here, as alluded to above, we find the children having freedom from the constraints of *having* to work out answers to particular closed questions; *having* to carry out particular actions, etc. In a (B) type situation attention is perforce on the *teacher*: her line of thought, what she wants etc., whereas in an (A) type situation attention is being drawn to the *situation* and to possible mathematical interests in it.

Two related points seem worthy of note here:

1   Sometimes, of course, a child *might* actually make a choice. So, for example, in the 'Circle arrangements' case-study the children each chose which numbers of spots they would shade in (p. 21).

2   Sometimes, not only might a child not be making a conscious choice from alternatives, he might do something without at first intending to draw out the particular features of it which are subsequently more consciously developed (see p. 103). As the teacher's role in this situation can be so crucial, there is further discussion of this sort of case in chapter 11.

KEEPING AN OPEN MIND

Often in the moves they make we find children setting themselves challenges which we would shy away from giving to them as tasks. So, for example, we find Matthew (5.06) working out what sixteen plus sixteen equal (p. 68); Helen (5.03) and Anne-Marie (5.08) attempting to find the total number of dots on their squares (p. 31); and Sam (5.03) counting all the shaded spots on his sheet (figure 3.16, p. 30).

The children often help each other to meet these challenges, sharing what they know. See, for example, how Sam (5.03) helped out Matthew (5.05) by supplying the words 'fifty', 'sixty', 'seventy' and 'eighty' when Matthew was not sure of them (p. 20).

The power of the children can be really astonishing, so much so that I often find that when teachers consider case-studies such as the ones in chapters 3 to 8, they are all too readily prepared to remark that such-and-such a child must have been special in some way since 'normal' 4 and 5 year olds would not be able to do such things.

Is it possible to become so blinkered in our acceptance of how children respond to tightly set tasks that we overlook their true capabilities?

HOW ACTIVE IS THE MATHEMATICS?

How does the idea of children participating in steering what happens link up with points about the mathematics itself? As has already been suggested at the start of this chapter, the taking of initiatives and being involved actively in mathematics are inextricably linked. In the last chapter we noted children engaging in a whole range of mathematical processes and items of content and, as is implicit from situations (A) and (B) (pp. 111–13, it is these entities which could feature solely as a result of direct leading by the teacher or through more of the children's own volition.

So, to consider just one more of the numerous available examples from the case-studies, in chapter 3 we find the children imposing their own rules. Jemma (5.04) decides that her two spots have to be next to one another (p. 23); Sam (5.03) keeps to his pattern (see figure 10.2) and keeps putting it in different orientations (as in figure 3.8); Ilona (5.04) repeats some of her arrangements and thus builds up a pattern (figure 3.4), etc. That they should engage in such processes was not stipulated by me – they started on these themselves.

You have probably already noticed that I led the children more in the 'Plates of biscuits' case-study (chapter 7) than in the rest of the episodes described in this book. The original seeds for the ideas which were then developed were of Ilona's (5.05) and Jemma's (5.05) making but I framed fairly tightly part of what ensued from these:

- The children read out the answers from Ilona's paper *because I had asked them to.*
- The children said what they noticed about the numbers they had found *because I had asked them to.*
- The children continued the sequence of numbers *because I had asked them to.*

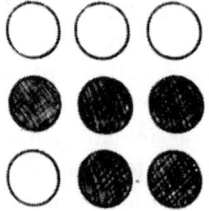

Figure 10.2 Sam's pattern

115

Would they have chosen to do any of these things had I not specifically asked them to? Would they ever have perceived such possibilities? Perhaps the children's required engagement in such activities here might lead to them choosing to do likewise on another occasion. Put more generally, perhaps sometimes constraining children to act in particular ways can serve to widen their perceptions of what it is fruitful to choose to do.

Your own examples of where putting constraints on an activity has actually seemed to widen children's possible choices later.

Given a process or item of content, there will often be a whole range of possible initiatives associated with it. So, for example, with 'counting' we might associate:

- deciding *to* count something;
- deciding *what* will be counted;
- deciding *how* to count something.

Some of these possible initiatives, centred on one process/item of content, may in a sense be prior to others. So, to continue with the above example, deciding *how* to count something suggests that one has already determined *to* count it. If a child has taken initiatives with one of these it does not mean that she has taken initiatives with the other.

So, the teacher might tell children to count something, but somehow invite them to decide how they are going to do so;

or:

children might suggest counting something, but the teacher then points to each of the objects in turn (perhaps they are arranged in a higgledy-piggledy fashion), counting with the children.

Because of the depth of removal from the imposition of the teacher they suggest, situations are interesting to watch where two or more of deciding to, deciding what, and deciding how are in the hands of the children. For instance, in the 'A stick of cubes' activity we find Joseph (4.10) himself coming up with the idea 'We could change that around a little bit, couldn't we?' (p. 80) and then actually finding a way of doing so. My only involvement in that part of the episode was to attend to what Joseph was doing.

It seems impossible to quantify in any way the children's depth of removal from the teacher's imposition, but sometimes I sense a greater gap than at other times. In particular there seems to be a distinction to be made between (a) Children taking initiatives/making a choice *within* what I perceived I had required them to do; and (b) Children taking initiatives/making a choice *beyond* or *other than* what I perceived I had required them to do. Some examples might help to clarify what I mean here:

(a) is the most usual in the case-studies. One specific instance was when Matthew (5.05), Jemma (5.04) and Sam (5.03) commented on the sorts of shapes in the circles sheet (p. 19). They were formulating and putting forward their own perceptions in response to being asked 'What can you say about what you've got?'

(b) is rarer and potentially more exciting in that it can suggest more originality of thought. An example occurred in the 'Number squares' activity. When I gave the children the little blank squares of card, I envisaged that they would use only the nine I gave them and put them in the three-by-three grids. Ben (5.05), however, had an unusual idea when putting dots on the cards: he decided to draw on one one, two twos, three threes, and four fours; this led to his deciding to use an extra square of card and extending his grid to accommodate it (p. 49).

You might find it interesting to go through some of the case-studies considering whether particular instances of the children's steering of the activities fit best into category (a) or (b) or neither.

It is situations such as (b) which can, of course, provide the teacher with a particular dilemma. For example, one might have involved all the children in carrying out a *particular* task at the beginning of a session with the intention of opening up possibilities for initiatives later: sometimes the later an explicit invitation for initiatives is given, the more possibilities the children can see. So, if a child deviates from the original task itself, this can set up considerable tensions for the teacher: should one interfere or not? There is no straightforward, definitive answer to such a question since much depends on individual circumstances, but the issue will be considered a little further in the next chapter.

We have to be careful in making judgements about the extent of a child's originality of thought. It is possible that a child is bringing to bear on his 'initiatives' something specific from what has happened before of which we are unaware. For example when Joseph (4.10) and Xanthe (4.10) suggested putting a blank/black cube at the end of the stick of six white and blue cubes so that it did not have to be counted (p. 75), it is possible, for instance, that they had recently been involved in looking at beads on part of an abacus and been told to make sure not to count the fixed piece at the bottom of the wire.

I do not mean to imply that there is anything wrong in utilising ideas learnt earlier. That would be ridiculous since making such connections between contexts is a vital part of learning, to be sought for and welcomed all the time. Rather, it seems important to note that the initiative-taking might not be as novel as one thinks at first, and that one is always going to have uncertainties about what, specifically, children are bringing to bear on the ideas they suggest. And even if one does know that a child has met

117

something before, one will not know how different it is for the child to bring this experience into a new context.

Sometimes we might also make the mistake of thinking that what a child is doing/suggesting goes beyond or counters what we have suggested (thus we might ascribe greater diversity than warranted by what happens). This was the case when Sam (5.04) suggested that ten could be made from four and six in the 'Plates of biscuits' activity (p. 67). At the time, I thought that the salient feature of what had preceded Sam's suggestion was trying to express a number using *two numbers the same* and that Sam had diverted from this. However, as remarked on p. 67, when I listened to a recording of the session afterwards, I realised that what I had actually *said* did not require equal sets at all.

I have already alluded to a distinction between children *intending* to do something and children acting in a way in which it is we, rather than they, who perceive certain features (see p. 114). Children often do vocalise their intentions in passing but, at other times, it can be difficult, if not impossible, to glean insights into what their purposes are. It is very dangerous to assume that we are correct in inferring a particular intention from an action: often another's behaviour can be interpreted in a whole variety of different ways. We might ask children why they have done something to see if we can gain any idea of whether it happened with intent or not. But it seems important to note here that our questioning could itself make a child feel she ought to have a reason, so she might actually make one up. A more neutral question such as 'What can you say about what you have been doing?' *might* be more revealing (but how would we know if it were?). A child could say anything, and might only give her reasons for doing something if she actually had any. But it still might cause a child to be explicit, using language that she had not used in her conception of the idea before, so the framing of an intention might now be crystallised much more definitely than it had been originally. On the other hand, she might choose not to discuss her reasons at all! This is not to argue against asking children such questions, far from it. Rather, it is meant to show how we need to be on our guard against ascribing intentions to children which, in fact, they did not have.

Are there other ways of trying to gain insights into children's intentions?

LINKS WITH OTHER CONCEPTS

You may have noticed that, so far in this analysis, I have not used terms such as 'creativity', or 'investigations', or 'discovery learning'. I have, in fact, avoided these on purpose. This is because each of them can carry with it overtones which do not necessarily fit what has happened. And because these words occur so frequently in educational contexts there is a danger that a reader might accept *my* usage of them without questioning their aptness here.

This is not the place to carry out detailed debates about these complex concepts, especially as excellent analyses occur elsewhere (see, for example, Haylock 1987 and Tammadge 1979). It does, however, seem important to draw attention to the few points which follow:

- Much of what has been written on creativity in a mathematical context, applies best to older children. For example, Krutetskii (1976) says that creativity in mathematics is seen in 'the independent formulation of uncomplicated mathematical problems, finding ways and means of solving these problems, the invention of proofs and theorems, the independent deduction of formulas, and finding original methods of solving nonstandard problems' (p. 68).

  We have to ask ourselves whether there is anything of relevance to 4 and 5 year olds in such discussions.

- A great deal of what has been written on creativity is also most applicable to *problem-solving*. This is true of the Krutetskii quote above and, to cite another example, it is evident in Westcott's (1978) claim that 'Creative teaching of mathematics ... means that both the teacher and the children pose meaningful problems in mathematics and explore a wide variety of methods for solving the problems. Finally, they identify many ways to express the solution or solutions they have selected' (p. 29).

  But what I have been reporting on are instances where children have participated in steering more open activities. To talk of a child solving a problem, however inventive he/she might be in doing so, is still to suggest that he/she is aiming to do something in particular.

- Sometimes authors are particularly concerned with discussing the creation of something for the first time, for example a mathematician conceiving a new type of structure or proving something which has never been proved before. See, for instance, Poincaré's description of his own creation of what he subsequently called 'Fuchsian functions' in Ghiselin (1952).

  But in talking about young children's initiatives, curiosity and discoveries, I am not thinking of creativity in such a sense.

- Sometimes the notion of 'creativity' is allied with that of 'giftedness'.

  But what I am writing about concerns children of all abilities.

- Often associated with the idea of assessing creativity are tests such as those devised by Getzels and Jackson in which, typically, the person being tested has to think up as many uses as he/she can for an object such as a paperclip. See, for example, Getzels and Jackson (1962).

  But obtaining a high score in such a test does not necessarily entail that a child will be particularly prominent in steering the direction of mathematical activities such as those described in the case-studies.

- The notion of 'discovery learning' places an emphasis on something being discovered.

  The notion of children participating in steering the direction of activities does not necessarily square with this. To make one's own suggestions is not necessarily to make a discovery.

- Often the term 'discovery learning' is applied to situations where the teacher has carefully planned a sequence of events which will guide children into finding out a particular thing. For example, Foster (1972) writes: 'The sequence is usually as follows: first, aims and objectives of the particular activity are thought out and documented. Then, learning experiences are devised which rely on a form of guided discovery, so that the final act of finding-out belongs to the child. These activities should be specifically designed to try to achieve the stated aims and objectives' (p. 6).

  But the situations I am describing allow for and encourage much more flexibility. There is much less of an emphasis on children following predetermined paths.

- Teachers often say such things as, 'I did an investigation with my children today'. Perhaps implicit in this is that tomorrow the children will return to their usual work on such topics as 'addition' etc.

  In writing about children carrying out their own mathematical thinking, I am talking about something which is much more all-pervasive. Work on all items of 'content' in syllabuses can itself come about through children's active participation in thinking mathematically (see chapter 9, p. 108).

- The title 'investigation' is most often applied to a situation where a child tackles a starting-point such as those listed in *Bounce to it!* (1984) etc.

  The sessions on which I have been reporting have not all arisen in such a way.

- Put in their less ossified form, creating, discovering, and investigating do most certainly have a part to play in an analysis of the children's personal engagement in mathematics. As examples, we can talk of Hayley (4.10) *creating* the squares within squares structure (p. 40); Ben (5.05) *discovering* that six can be made from one, two and three (p. 47); and Joseph (4.10) *investigating* how the stick of three blue and three white cubes could be changed round (p. 80).

I found it worthwhile to consider the applicability of these words to other incidents in the case-studies.

120

I started this chapter with a comment about how it is intimately connected with the previous chapter. A similar remark is now required about the next chapter. Obviously, my own role in the sessions described in chapters 3 to 8 was thoroughly intertwined with both the mathematics in which the children became involved and the active manner in which they did so: they and I constantly influenced each other's perceptions and actions. Nevertheless there are some specific things to be said about the teachers' role and these will be discussed under a separate heading.

11

THE TEACHER'S ROLE

OPENING REMARKS

Whilst I was engaged in this project with young children, I became aware of various features of the way in which I act which seemed to be significant in encouraging the children to participate in steering their own mathematical activities. This chapter seeks to highlight and discuss those features.

It would not be appropriate to imagine that I can give a definitive account of what to do. The facets of my role brought out into the open here are not meant to serve as generalisations. There is no way in which I can say that, given such and such a situation, I would always respond in a particular way. As every teacher knows, the complexity of life in the classroom is immense. We operate within an exceedingly intricate and ever-evolving web of human relationships, weighing up situations at lightning speed and continually making on-the-spot decisions. The elements within a situation are often conflicting, in any case: for example, we might aim to involve all children in suggesting their own ideas but end up putting constraints on some individuals in order to encourage others who are more reticent. The features of my role discussed in this chapter would be more aptly described as 'non-unique'[1] rather than as 'general' attributes.

To try to lay bare what these non-unique features are proved to be a far from straightforward matter. We bring to every situation a wealth of pre-conceived notions and background assumptions which are part-and-parcel of the way we act. Trying to tease these out is certainly impossible when we are enmeshed in face-to-face situations with children: we are caught in the 'living intentionality' of what is happening (Schutz 1972). But even when taking opportunities to reflect on events after they have happened, we are still caught within our own perceptual frameworks. In order to help present other perspectives, a number of people[2] have watched me working with children either 'live' or on video tape recordings and numerous others have listened to audio tape recordings. Their viewpoints have included a whole host of comments and questions which have helped me to reflect on and modify my own awarenesses.

What I have written is not intended to be prescriptive. For example, some facets of my actions may not fit well with another teacher's personality. I hope, however, that it provides food for thought and helps to stimulate ideas about widening/altering choices for action in the classroom.

I have found it useful to focus my attention on six main areas: the opening of an activity; planning sessions; seeking and using children's ideas; aspects of the teacher's authority; putting children at ease; and involving children in complex and sometimes conflicting ideas. These are not meant to seem like disparate elements: they merely served as helpful centres of accretion in my thinking. The points discussed under the headings all intertwine with one another.

The points all relate to the 4 and 5 year olds with whom I worked. Readers used to working with older children might find some of them familiar but it seems important to include as many as possible here since leaving something out could convey the impression that I believe it to be irrelevant to this young age group.

Trying to analyse what my role has been in sessions was very time-consuming at first. It took quite a while to decide which sorts of actions it might be profitable to continue, which ones I could/should attempt to refine, and so on. As the children carried out more and more activities, however, the analysis became much less tedious and the decision-making became easier.

Before concentrating on the main body of this chapter, you might find it useful to consider the following list. This identifies some of my underlying assumptions which might help provide a backdrop to the rest of the discussions.

Some personal axioms

- No matter how 'far behind the others' I view particular children, *all* children starting in a reception class already have tremendous capabilities.
- Children often show surprising powers, going well beyond my expectations. I try not to put any ceiling on my view of what they can do.
- Children actively seek to understand the world. They explore, try things out, etc. I trust in their ability to learn.
- Children's perceptions are continually changing. Reinterpretation is essential in learning. Any insights I think I gain into a child's knowledge and abilities I try to view as transient.
- We often benefit from formulating our ideas through talking with others.
- There are countless ways of building up knowledge, not just one preferred route. To think of mathematics as a hierarchical subject can be misleading. The order put on concepts and skills in mathematics schemes might seem appropriate to the particular teacher/author concerned, but

might not square with the thinking of the children who use the scheme. Children need opportunities to build up their own pathways.

- Just because one can demonstrate that, say, 'sets' are logically prior to 'number',[3] this need not have implications for learning and teaching.
- A too-ready acceptance of developmental theories (for example, Piaget's theory of intellectual development) can be very misleading, limiting one's expectations of what children can do and giving explanations when alternative interpretations are, in fact, possible.
- Inexplicitness, dead-ends, ambiguity and confusion are often necessary precursors to learning. Children gain from the struggle of trying to become clearer, trying to simplify, etc. and obtain great personal satisfaction from having 'sorted it out'.
- Children view things differently from me and from each other. Communication is far from straightforward and is at least two-way.

THE START

Some pseudo-principles

The start of a session plays a vital part in establishing an atmosphere for the whole of the session. When planning, I give a lot of thought to how to begin, not just centring this on the idea itself but also considering points like what I might actually say to the children. The following have evolved as significant facets of my thinking:

1   It seems important for the children to work on something with which they can quickly engage. If wordy explanations dominate the beginning of a session, children might all too easily feel that the scene has been set for the rest of the session: nothing would suggest that the 'teacher passing something on' role will not continue as usual.

2   The idea should be accessible to all members of the group. If it is not, then this is likely to make some children feel insecure immediately and the teacher may be left with no alternative other than to adopt the role of 'explainer'. On the other hand, restrictions imposed on the opening activity should be viewed as temporary so that there is potential for children to set themselves challenges.

For example, at the start of the 'Number squares' activity (chapter 5), I gave the children sets of only one dot, two dots and three dots on the cards, but this was not a permanent restriction. Giving the children blank squares later on led to a variety of pupil-set challenges.

3   Starting from a context which makes 'human sense' is important for encouraging young children to feel they can participate in controlling what is happening (see the references in chapter 9, p. 100 to Donaldson's work).

124

For example, 'things getting in a mess and needing sorting out' (see the example discussed on p. 109) is likely to make more human sense than the 'false concretisation' of drawing Venn diagrams.

4   Building in a rich variety of possibilities into the opening situation can provide potential for children to structure what happens. For example, in planning the 'A stick of cubes' activity. I saw opportunities for the children to do such things as:

(a) correct the situation somehow, maybe changing the 'hat' or maybe changing the number of cubes;
(b) change the order of the cubes, perhaps making more of a pattern with them;
(c) compare the number of blue and white cubes and make similar length sticks but with different numbers of blue and white cubes in them;
(d) change the number of colours being used.

5   Using children's own ideas from previous sessions emphasises the importance one is giving to the children's initiatives. See pp. 138–49 for further discussion of this.

6   Opening remarks can so easily be off-putting. 'Today we are going to do some counting' could sound exciting to some but boring to others or even posing a threat of the 'I've been here before and I wasn't very good at it then' feeling. It also circumscribes the content, giving no scope for the children's own perceptions.

Generating the start

The beginnings of fruitful mathematical activities often arise spontaneously, perhaps through the children's 'play'; or through their bringing in something to show to the other children; or through the need for some sort of organisation such as splitting into teams for physical education; and so on. The possibilities are endless. Furthermore, when children are actively engaged in coming up with their own ideas in a session, these are often not exhausted at the time and can serve as the beginnings of other sessions (see point (5), above, and p. 145. But what about occasions when one specifically plans the start of a session oneself?

It is possible to buy books of what have tended to become known as 'starting-points' (though, actually, precious few contain ideas suitable for young infants).[4] A danger in using such a starting-point is that one might be tempted to pass it on in the same form as it is written in the book, overlooking some of the factors listed in the previous section. These ideas for sessions can become just as ossified as the items of content in a syllabus.

So how do I decide on the beginnings of sessions?

125

Stimulating thought

Sometimes I do use ideas from booklets etc., but not usually in their given form. I tend to use them more as a stimulus to my own thinking. As an example, this is a record of such thinking around a starting-point when preparing an activity for a group of 5 year olds:

I can see potential in this idea from *Bounce To It!* (see figure 11.1). I could link it with the work the children on the back table have been doing on strips of squares. I *will* make a sheet of shapes, as suggested. It could look like this ... (see figure 11.2).

4. Flags 1

You have a red pen and a green pen.

Use them to colour flags like this:

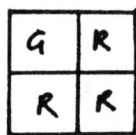

This one is a 'good' flag:

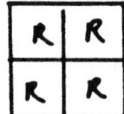

But this one isn't:

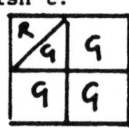

You must colour <u>whole</u> squares.

How many different flags can you colour?

Now try using a blue pen as well.

(Children will have to define 'different' for themselves. For example are these two different or not?

You must colour whole squares.

Note: A Banda sheet of shapes may help.

Figure 11.1 The basic idea in *Bounce To It!* from which I worked

Source: Hatch, G. (1984) *Bounce To It! A Collection of Investigations and Problems for Infants*, Manchester, Manchester Polytechnic (with permission).

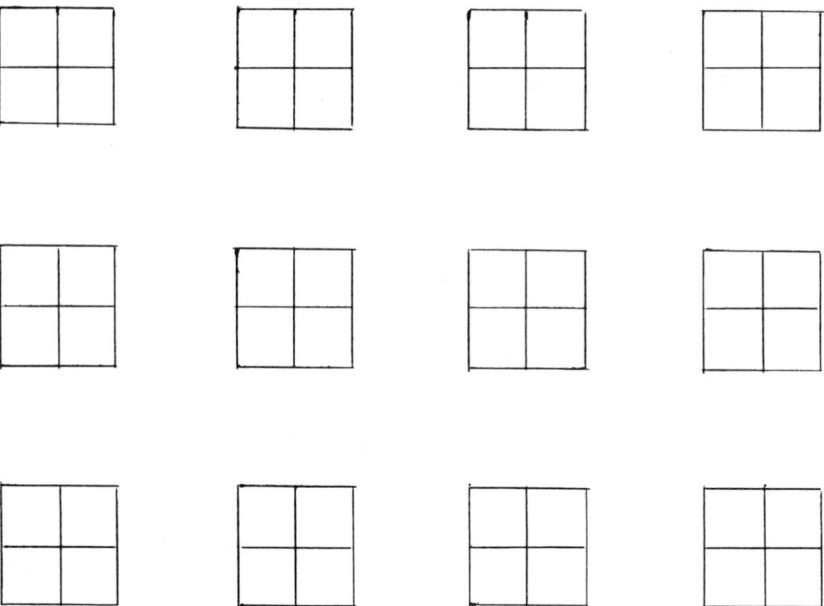

Figure 11.2 My sheet of shapes

It now occurs to me that just showing this to the children could be a starting-point in itself. The children might make spontaneous comments about the sheet or, if they do not, I could ask 'What can you say about this?' So I will not mention anything about colouring at this point.

The children might later decide for themselves that colouring the sheet would be a good activity. If they do not, I could say something like 'Perhaps you'd like to have a go at colouring in the sheet?' I will not necessarily refer to the shapes themselves as 'flags' but will wait to see if the children call them anything (simply 'squares' or 'windows' perhaps?), then use that label myself.

I will not impose the colouring of whole squares restriction. The children might make links with the activities we have been carrying out recently where 'halves' have come to the fore. If some do colour in parts of squares and others do not, this will also provide an opportunity subsequently for them to think in terms of how they are using different rules. That could pave the way for more conscious decisions about limitations etc. Similarly, as suggested in the book, I will leave the way open for them to define which shapes count as 'different' from others.

What about using other such starting-points as a stimulus to thinking?

127

Adapting ideas

Sometimes the starting-points on which I centre my thinking have been intended for older children but are amenable to adaptation for 4 and 5 year olds. For example, the following shows some exploration behind the preparation of the 'Number squares' activity (chapter 5):

The exercise shown in Figure 11.3 has proved to be very fruitful as a starting-point with older children.[5]

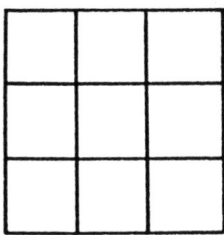

Figure 11.3 The puzzle invited the children to 'Arrange the numbers 4, 4, 4, 5, 5, 5, 6, 6, 6 in the square so that each row, column, and diagonal adds up to 15'

Can I transform it for use with my reception children?

As the idea stands, addition plays a prominent part. Perhaps I could change it into a *counting* activity? Instead of using numerals, each number could be represented by a set of dots. The dots could be on little pieces of card for the children to move round on a three by three grid. Then the children would not need to keep rubbing things out.

Using sets of four, five and six dots would mean that the children are expected to count up to fifteen which might prove difficult for some at the start. I could make up sets of one, two and three dots instead. The children could later choose their own numbers of dots to go on blank cards.

It could still be too difficult for the children actually to *aim* at making a particular total at the start, even if this total is now six and not fifteen. I will not mention totals at all; the children can put the sets of dots in their grids how they like at first. They might notice all sorts of things about their arrangements. I can draw attention to finding some of the totals once the children have filled in some squares. And there is still no need for the children subsequently to have to aim for particular totals, nor to end up with all the same totals, though they might well become involved in setting some such challenges themselves.

What about adapting other starting-points originally intended for older children?

As in the above example, transforming ideas so that they can be centred on counting is a strategy which can often be used when considering starting-points which would be too advanced as they stand.

The syllabus

Sometimes I start explicitly from the syllabus and think how I can enliven one or more of the items on it. The following is one example of how I have adapted the syllabus.

The syllabus refers to 'Recognising and finding half of objects'. As one activity in connection with this I could give the children a sheet of shapes; discuss with them how to split one of the shapes in half; then ask them to split the rest similarly. But, beyond deciding where to divide the shapes, there is little scope for initiatives here. The activity is simply the completion of a teacher-imposed worksheet, with little call for thinking beyond the 'how can I get it finished' kind. How could it be opened up?

The children have recently been working with logic blocks. Perhaps they could choose some of these to draw round and find half the resulting shapes? This would provide opportunities for such things as:

- structuring, for example some children might decide to work with each of the small squares;
- finding out that half of a small triangle can look the same as half of a larger triangle;
- comparing what they are doing and commenting on equivalences and differences;
- finding that the same shape can be split in half in a number (a never ending number?) of different ways;
- working out a strategy for exhausting all the different sorts of shapes.

What other activities would enliven 'Recognising and finding half of objects'?

What about starting from other items on the syllabus and trying to enliven them?

Worksheets

Sometimes I take already prepared worksheets or workcards, including ones from published schemes, and think how the ideas in them could be 'twisted' to provide more opportunities for children's initiatives. This was how the activity described in chapter 7 arose. The twist here was to leave the 'plates' empty on the class teacher's original worksheets and invite the children to put in their own numbers of 'biscuits'.

Consider twisting the ideas on some commercially produced worksheets or work-cards, or even on your own.

It often takes surprisingly little effort to turn a routine task into something over which children have greater control. For example:

A closed activity: A group of children are given a box of cubes and a strip of paper like that in figure 11.4.

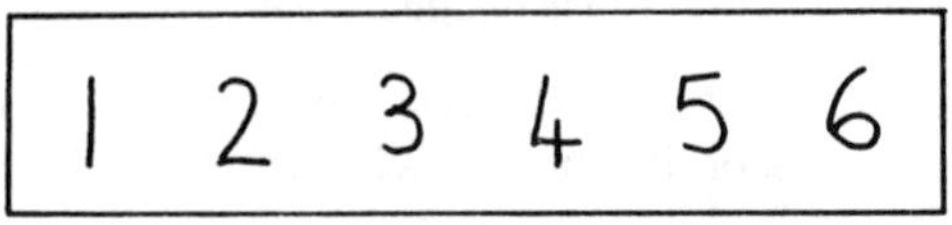

Figure 11.4 The strip of paper

For each numeral they have to count out the appropriate number of cubes; put them together in a stick; and stand the stick on the numeral.

A more open activity: The children are given a box of cubes and a pot containing little squares of paper with a numeral on each. There are several copies of each numeral. The children can *choose* a numeral from the pot; count out the appropriate number of cubes; and put them together in a stick; then keep repeating the activity. This opens up possibilities such as the following:

- some children might investigate which numerals they have in the pot, perhaps looking for the highest number or the lowest number, or seeing how many of a particular number there are, or comparing how many there are two or more numerals, etc.;
- some children might decide to structure what they are doing, searching for the numerals in order or searching for several copies of the same numeral, etc.;
- some children might consciously decide whether or not to put the numerals back in the pot each time, some children might decide to make a record of the numeral they have used each time by writing it on a piece of paper by the side of the appropriate stick.

And the situation could be opened up even further (later?) by the inclusion of some blank squares, for the children to choose which numerals are to be written on them.

Using restrictions

I sometimes involve children in opening activities such as the following:

1 Some children are given a set of three colouring pencils and invited to colour in a piece of paper with six-by-six squares on it. This was the start of the activity described in chapter 4.
2 Some children are given a set of three colouring pencils and piles of cut-out outline drawings of three different sorts of fish. They are invited to colour the fish and stick them on a piece of paper which they are to pretend is a 'fish tank'.
3 Some children are given sets of triangles which have been cut out of gummed paper and are invited to stick ten of them in a line on a piece of

paper. There are four different types of triangle and two colours of gummed paper.

4   Some children are given an outline drawing of a Christmas tree and piles of three different types of shapes to be stuck on the tree as 'decorations'. There are two colours of pencils available for them to colour the decorations. This was the start of the activity described in chapter 6.

These have in common a restriction on the number of colours to be used and a restriction on the objects children are to work with. Ironically, the very imposition of such restrictions can pave the way for a whole host of mathematical developments. These might arise as children are working on the activity or may be brought out of discussions about what the children have completed. There are endless possibilities for creating situations like this.

Try making some up!

Configurations

Sometimes I think up a configuration to show to the children, inviting them to draw out and develop their own perceptions of it. The sheet of circles in chapter 3 and the stick of cubes in chapter 8 are examples of such configurations. Each provides a variety of possibilities for comments and actions. Again, there is an enormous number of ways of creating sheets like this.

Figure 11.5 gives one other example. What about your own ideas?

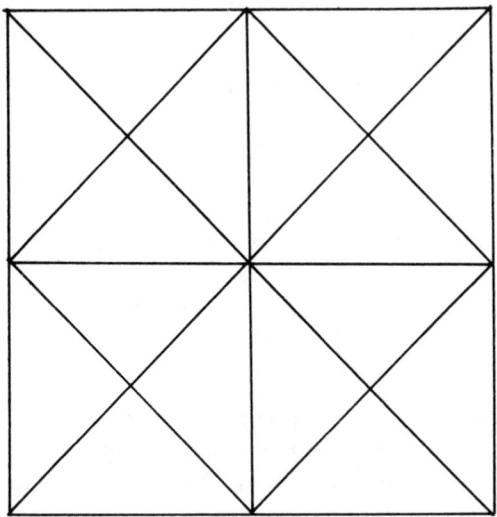

Figure 11.5 One idea for a sheet

Inspiration

So far, it may sound as if I always adopt definite strategies for generating starting-points. There is somehow a mechanical feel to what I have written, as if there is an automatic recipe for making up fruitful ideas. This is not the case in practice.

In particular, let me say something further about hitting on the seeds for the ideas. This is difficult to express and is perhaps best conveyed at first implicitly through a couple of examples:

1   One of the teachers has put a large polystyrene snowman in the hall with an invitation for anyone in the school to write a story about him. The reception children are fascinated by him. I find myself wondering if there is any potential for mathematics here. He has six black buttons but just to count those would be trivial. And we cannot take them off to do anything with them. But . . . if I made some drawings of the snowman . . .

> . . . there could be blank buttons on those, to be coloured with a limited set of colours, with the potential for discussion about number bonds to six . . .;

> . . . or no buttons at all, with the potential for each child to decide how many to put on and we could compare different children's work . . .

2   I have just received some Christmas cards. The picture on one is of a group of children around a crib. In the foreground is a pile of presents. I catch myself wondering if there are enough presents for each child to give to the baby. I am suddenly aware that there is potential here for an activity. I could show a group of children this card and ask them to talk about it. And what about other cards? I hunt and find:

- some with clear-cut groupings (pictures of the twelve days of Christmas etc.);
- some with not such clear-cut groupings (a village in the snow etc.);
- some whose main feature is just a small number of a particular type of object (four robins etc.);
- some whose main feature is a large number of a particular type of object (baubles on a Christmas tree etc.);
- some with the same type of objects on them but in different numbers on each card (one card with three bells on it, another with one bell on it, another with five bells on it, etc.);

. . . and so on. There are many opportunities for discussion here. In both cases I have not consciously sat down and thought 'Let me make up an idea!' Something in the continual flux of events has caught my attention and has started to serve as a focus for the generation of an idea. The very nature of this sort of occurrence means that I cannot prescribe rules for it to happen. It is very much part and parcel of the way I act. But suppose it is not for you? Perhaps one could consciously start to accustom oneself to trying to see mathematical potential in the world that surrounds us.

For example, look around the classroom. Is there any potential for mathematics? What about in the grouping of the chairs at the tables? The windows? The floor? The paint palettes? The books on the shelf? Could any of these form the germ of an idea?

ON PLANNING AHEAD

In deciding on an opening activity, I set in train thoughts on ways in which it might continue. In a sense I cannot separate the beginning from the potential development: when I choose to start a session with a particular activity it is because I forsee the likelihood of fruitful ideas emerging from it.

The danger is that these foreseen possibilities actually restrict what happens in practice. I may become so caught up in my own expectations that I fail to see the emergence of different ideas from the children, or I stifle them because I am so enmeshed in seeing the value in mine. How do I try to guard against this?

The situation is complex. This is a first go at expressing what I think I do: I strive not to have a *rigid* plan in mind ('After they have done _____ then I will say _____ and involve them in _____', etc.). I have referred to 'foreseen possibilities' above and this is what the items in my planning are – *possibilities*. When I am actually working with the children and they seem purposefully engaged, I try to focus away from my earlier thoughts on how the situation might develop and concentrate on what the children actually seem to be doing and suggesting. However, my earlier ideas can be brought into the open if, for example, providing a new focus to the session feels appropriate.

Now let me add more to this description, firstly through reflection on an example.

Circle arrangements

The planning

This was my planning for the first part of what has been written up in chapter 3. A lot of this was just in my mind at the time. What I actually wrote down can be seen in figure 11.6. Below is a development of my early ideas. The numbers are just to help with the analysis. The roman and italic type-faces distinguish between my potential actions and the children's potential actions.

1 Give out sheet.
2 *They might comment immediately.*

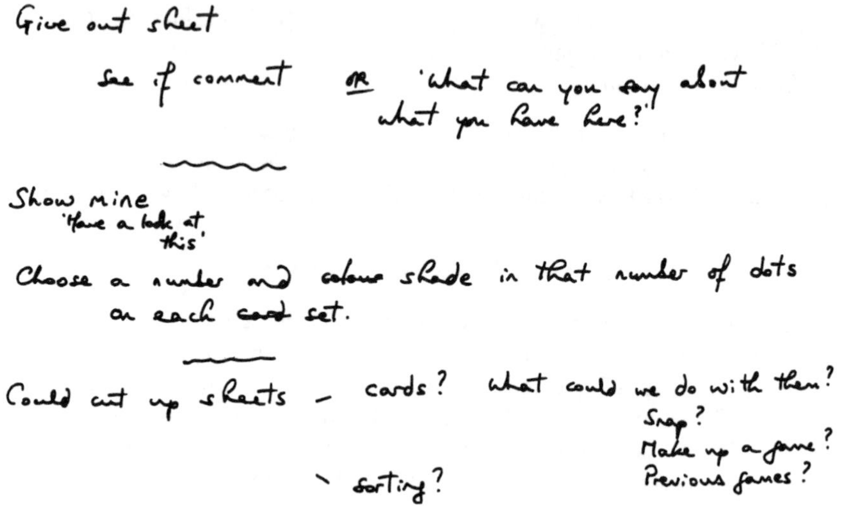

Give out sheet

    See if comment <u>or</u> 'what can you say about
                  what you have here?'

Show mine
  'Have a look at
     this'
Choose a number and colour shade in that number of dots
    on each card set.

Could cut up sheets — cards? what could we do with them?
                                  Snap?
                                  Make up a game?
           sorting?   Previous games?

Figure 11.6 My early ideas

3 If not, say something like 'What can you say about what you have here?'
4 *They might become involved in counting; comparing; noticing differences and equivalences (three circles across, three circles down; nine sets of nine circles, etc.); describing shapes; naming shapes; talking in terms of 'sets', etc.*
5 *They might also make some suggestions for what to do with the sheet (colouring the circles etc.).*

Possibilities for development:

6 I could show them my sheet on which I have shaded sets of three spots (figure 3.2, page 21), saying, 'Have a look at this.'
7 *They might become involved in number recognition; counting; comparing; noticing equivalences and differences, etc.*
8 I could invite them to choose their own number and shade in that number of circles on each set in a different way.
9 *They would be involved in starting from a particular number; finding an appropriate set; thinking about equivalences and differences. They might also compare their numbers of circles with those of other children in the group; find out how many circles are left unshaded in each set; find that this unshaded number is always the same; build some sort of system into what they are doing, etc.*
10 I could invite them to cut up the sheets along the straight lines and ask them what they could do with the little rectangles.
11 *They might suggest using them like cards to play a game, for example 'Snap' which would involve comparing numbers; thinking about equivalences and differences; recognising that different configurations can still have the same*

number of constituent parts. If they muddle up the rectangles they might want to sort them out later.

Are there any other possibilities?

What happened in practice?

I started with (1). The children did *not* comment immediately (2), so I asked 'What can you say about what you've got?' (This had the same meaning as (3).)

They did become involved in much from (4) and more besides. I had *not* anticipated Matthew wanting to count *all* the circles and felt a little uneasy as he made this suggestion. Thoughts flitted through my mind like would it matter if he could not cope? But I restrained myself from stopping him and what followed was very fruitful.

They did not make any suggestions about colouring the circles (5). When there was a lull in their comments I showed them my second sheet (6) saying 'Have a look at what I've done.' They made some comments, touching on some of (7), but this did not last long, so I went on to (8). They became involved in much of (9) and, again, more besides. I made no stipulation about each set being different as I had intended in (8) as I simply did not remember that this had been part of my original idea. This paved the way for some children patterning, for example where Ilona repeated her configurations (figure 3.4, page 23).

I asked some of the children to complete more than one sheet when they finished the first one quickly. I had not thought of doing this when planning.

Number (10) did not feature: the session was entirely taken up with the above. I decided, however, that it might form an appropriate start to the next session. The children did *not* suggest the cards idea (11) and the pieces did not become muddled so there was no subsequent sorting either. I was surprised by Matthew's idea of gluing the rectangles on a piece of paper, and my exclamation 'We've just cut them up!' was an immediate reaction to that. The germ of the idea continued, however, and opened up fruitfully. I had not had this development in mind at all.

What other issues are there to be discussed in connection with this example? My potential actions detailed in the plan could be viewed as potential turning-points: if used, they would become new focii for attention. They serve as mental sign-posts which could spark off a change of direction. My preparation for a session consists mainly in alerting myself to possible turning-points.

In practice, what the children do often makes it unnecessary for me to put into motion such ideas. Sometimes this is because the children become involved in the activities through their own volition. Sometimes it is because the children become so involved in things like (4) that this takes over the rest of the session.

Sometimes, however, I have to use pre-planned turning-points even when it seems that what the children have already become involved in could continue profitably. This is mainly when I need to leave a group so that I can work with others. So, for example, even if the children's response to (7) had looked as if it could have lasted for longer, I might have had to have switched to (8), as this provides space for me to be elsewhere.

There is an order implicit in the potential turning-points. Number (10) could not happen without (8) happening first etc. Often, however, I do not place an order on any ideas for the development of an activity. For example, when planning the 'A stick of cubes activity' (chapter 8) I had thought of various potential turning-points to re-focus attention if necessary, but there was no need at all for them to be in any particular order.

Issues about planning

However much I intend to concentrate on what children actually seem to be doing and suggesting, my earlier planning does sometimes get in the way. In particular, my expectations of what *might* happen can so distort my perceptions of what *is* happening that I misconstrue what is actually the case.

For example, on one occasion I gave each child in a group of six 5 year olds a piece of paper with three squares on it (see figure 11.7). I also gave them three cubes: one red, one blue and one green. I asked them to put their cubes on the squares, then to put them on differently, then differently again, then differently again, etc. In planning the activity I thought that this start might involve the children in seeing a need to record what they were doing because it would be difficult to remember the arrangements. In practice, having made three arrangements some of the children did show signs of unease. As examples, Ricky (5.10) said, 'I don't know what to do to make a pattern ... I can't do another pattern', and Katie (5.09) said, 'It's too hard because you've already done the pattern.' Noticing the unease and anticipating difficulty in remembering I said, 'It's difficult to remember, isn't it, which patterns you've done and which patterns you haven't done', and went on to encourage the children to think how they could help themselves remember. When listening to a tape of this session and looking at the

Figure 11.7 The three-squared paper

children's subsequent records of their cube arrangements, however, it occurred to me that the children had probably not meant what I thought at the time. They (or some of them) might have been concentrating on moving a particular colour cube, realised they had put it in each of the three spaces and thought they had exhausted all the possible arrangements. My remark, 'It's difficult to remember . . .' probably did not square with their thinking at all.

Do you have any of your own examples of where planning has actually inhibited what happened or distorted your perceptions?

There is no point in saying that one must watch that such things do not happen. We cannot stop ourselves having expectations: they are part and parcel of on-going thinking. Nevertheless, being *aware* that expectations can distort our perceptions seems important. Perhaps we can become more attuned to asking ourselves continually such questions as 'Does what I think here actually match up with what X is thinking?' We can strive to keep more of an open mind even if we do not always succeed.

I have spoken of my (conquered) feeling of unease when Matthew started to count all the circles on his sheet. Here he was taking something (counting) further than I had envisaged when planning the session. Sometimes children become involved in something quite significantly different from what I had originally intended and I have to make a decision about whether to let them continue or not.

For example, this was the case when Sam (5.04) became involved in thinking which pairs of different numbers combined to give ten (p. 67). As is implicit in my account of that session, I had foreseen the whole activity being centred on finding which pairs of *equal* numbers gave certain other numbers, but Sam departed from that. I made an on the spot decision, however, not to stop him. Sam was a very shy and sensitive boy who could easily have felt 'quashed'.

Such decisions are necessarily spur of the moment ones. Many factors other than a child's temperament might influence them. For example, one might have it in mind that everyone conforming at the start of a particular activity could lead to wider opportunities for initiatives later (cf. p. 117 and p. 140).

Sometimes I feel under quite a lot of pressure to stop children departing from ideas which featured in my planning. Unfortunately, it is easy to think in terms of 'The syllabus won't be covered'; 'The situation might get out of control'; or 'It is more important for them to be working on what I had intended', etc. However, I believe we often delude ourselves if we think in such a way.

If you experience some of these worries, you might ask yourself whether they will definitely prove to be the case. Could the departure actually be profitable?

I am aware that I often make use of what might be called 'chance happenings' in sessions. By definition, these are things which are unplanned.

For example, on one occasion Ilona (5.02), Sam (5.01), Jemma (5.02) and Matthew (5.03) were looking at some discs with spots on either side. At one point they became involved in seeing how many of the discs had just one spot on one side and disagreed about their answers. In the middle of the children's counting and arguments one of the discs fell on to Ilona's lap by accident. Suddenly she noticed it and put it back on the table. I seized on this, drawing attention to the added complexity to the situation! This led to some of the children becoming involved in more complicated number work than I would have envisaged possible.

Such chance happenings are all part and parcel of the situation as it is developing to the children. It seems much more natural to make use of these happenings than to ignore them in favour of items from one's earlier planning.

Because I do not stick rigidly to a lesson plan, the 'same' start to a session often leads to different things with different children.

For example, when I showed Ilona (5.09), Sam (5.08), Rachel (5.07) and Matthew (5.10) the seven cubes with the 'six' hat stick, they became involved in very different activities from those that Joseph (4.10), Xanthe (4.10), Cirwyn (5.00) and Leanne (5.00) had done (chapter 8). They decided very quickly to take one cube off the stick to give them the correct number, hardly debating this at all. Then they focused on the fact that there remained three white cubes and three blue cubes. They wanted to make other sticks with equal numbers of cubes in them and the session became centred on doubling and, eventually, trebling.

You might find it interesting to consider the beginning of one or more of the other sessions from chapters 4 to 8 and think how they might have developed differently.

When working with a second group of children, I have to try to avoid pushing the activities in the directions pursued by the first group of children. This is not always very easy because of the expectations one has acquired but it seems important if one is not to impose an unnecessary straight-jacket on the session.

Repeating the start of a session with different children can increase one's own aware-ness of possibilities. For someone fearful of not being able to see such possibilities, this can be an important way to gain confidence.

SEEKING AND USING CHILDREN'S IDEAS

The whole of this book is centred around ways of encouraging children to develop their own mathematical ideas, but there are some specific things to be said under this sub-heading.

I frequently start episodes by asking children such questions as 'What can you tell me about this?', 'What can you say about what you've got?', etc. Or I might even show them something without asking a question about it at all. (See the start of chapters 3 and 8 for such examples of the beginning of sessions.) Open invitations like this explicitly call for children to frame their own responses. The emphasis is on the children forming and expressing their own perceptions. Not only do I often *start* episodes with what I think of as open questions, I often also ask them about what the children are in the middle of doing or have competed. (See p. 23 and p. 33 for just two of the many examples in the case-studies.)

Consider this, however:

> MB: Can you think of any way to help us remember which ones we've had?
>
> Joseph (5.0): Write them down.

What Joseph was working on is of no significance here. Although I could see the potential for several different answers to my question, Joseph might have viewed it in much more of a 'closed' sense. To him, writing down might have been the only possibility. Moreover, he might have viewed what I said as a 'teacher trying to illicit a particular response' type of question ('We were doing writing yesterday so that must be the answer'). Just because we see questions as open, this does not mean that children always do.

Of course, closed questions can be asked on purpose. So, for example, a question such as 'How many lines are there like this of yellow?' (chapter 4, p. 38) is not encouraging Lianne (5.03) to tease out and comment on a feature herself, but is looking for a definite answer. Even here, however, the closed question is about something in which Lianne had already been very personally involved: she had formed the structure herself. Moreover, some questions which might seem closed on the surface end up allowing for flexibility in responses. For example, when I asked Lianne how many sets of red squares there were in the first six by six square she had coloured (p. 38), I anticipated 'two' as the correct answer, but when she replied 'three' it seemed important not to dismiss this as wrong but to give her space to explain her thinking.

Focusing ideas

Frequently, once children have been engaged in something for a little while, I feel it is important to put them in a position of having to formulate their own ideas for continuing. For example, after the children had been working with the cards with sets of one, two and three dots on them in the 'Number squares' activity, I gave them *blank* cards so that they could decide on their own numbers of dots (cf. p. 124, point (2)).

When I first worked with young infants, I used to ask them questions like, 'What can we do next?' but I found that they often responded with suggestions which were out of the local context I had in mind. Of course, that was significant in itself. They said things such as, 'Hang up the coats!' (the teacher had grumbled about the state of the cloakroom at break time!), 'Do some painting!', etc. Hence I tried to find ways of giving them some freedom but within what I saw as the mathematical situation. Unfortunately, imposing such bounded freedom means that other potential changes within the situation might be cut off too. To continue with the 'Number squares' example, having been given the blank cards the emphasis for the children is on changing the number of dots and not on such things as changing the size or shape of the original three by three grid. Once involved in changing one feature of an activity, however, children often seem to think of other features to change too. So, in the 'Number squares' activity, we find Ben (5.05) deciding to change the number of blank cards to use and hence altering his grid as well.

There are, of course, possibilities between the open-to-any-context question, 'What can we do next?' and situations such as the provision of blank cards. For example, in the 'Circle arrangements' activity, when I asked the group what they could do with the little rectangles (p. 28), this was not tying the children down to altering an already worked-on feature of a situation, they had to think afresh, though still within the context of working with the pieces.

Children taking the initiative

Sometimes children can make up their own examples for tasks, either to give to someone else to do or for their own completion. For example, a group of children had been working from cards such as the one shown in figure 11.8. They had to build up the same sequences of colours as given, first using plastic cubes, then copying the sequence on to squared paper. Giving them some blank card and squares of gummed paper, I invited the children to make up their own cards.

As noted in chapter 10 (p. 114), children will often set themselves or other children harder tasks than we would normally set them ourselves. So for example, on a later occasion than that described in chapter 7, Ilona (5.03) set Sam (5.02) a really complicated 'plates of biscuits' sheet which Sam was none the less able to complete (see figure 11.9)!

When children ask questions such as, 'Shall I do this?' or, 'How can I …?' I often turn these back to them, asking 'What do you think?', seeing if they can make their own decisions or find their own ways of doing something. Sometimes they do not ask a question directly but imply from their comments that they are seeking direction, and again, if possible I try to turn the situation round so that the children are involved in taking the initiative

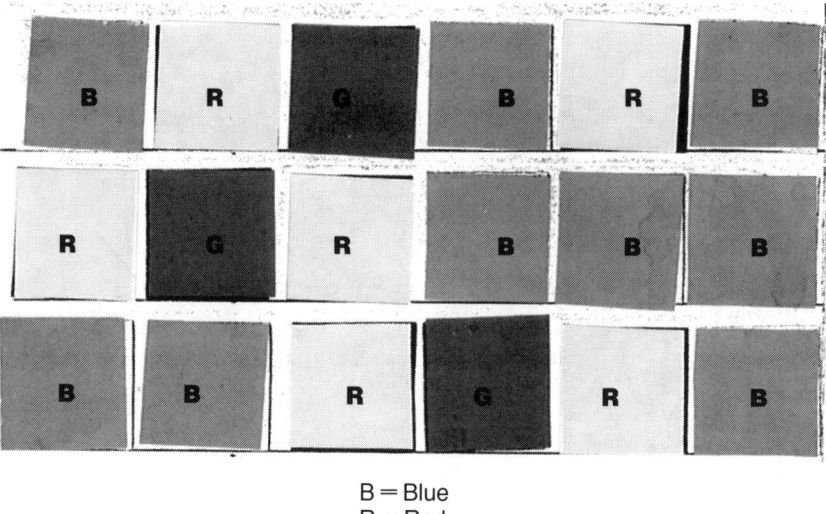

B = Blue
R = Red
G = Green

Figure 11.8 The card from which the children worked

themselves. For example, when Jemma (5.04) called across to me that she had shaded six spots instead of four on her circles sheet (p. 22), it seemed that she might be expecting me to tell her what to do. Rather than making any suggestion myself, however, I asked what we could do about it and Matthew (5.05) and Ilona (5.04) had an idea.

Sometimes, what a child could do to rectify a situation might seem obvious to *us* but this does not mean we have to supply the suggestion. In fact, if we wish to develop some measure of autonomy it is at such points that we have to ask, 'Will my intervention be helpful in the long run?'

Encouraging development

So far, I have been discussing instances where children have been required *explicitly* to formulate their own ideas. Often, however, encouraging the development of ideas is far more subtle than this.

As an example of what I mean, let us return to the discussion of the cards example started above. Many of the cards which the childen first produced themselves were like the ones they had been working from at first, in that there was no obvious pattern to the colours of the squares. In a few cards, however, I noticed some patterning. See the top line of Carlly's (5.01) for example, in figure 11.10. This patterning might have *arisen* by accident but I asked the children to talk about each other's cards and several then saw patterns in them. Patterning subsequently became a feature which children incorporated on purpose in their next cards. Indeed, some of the patterning

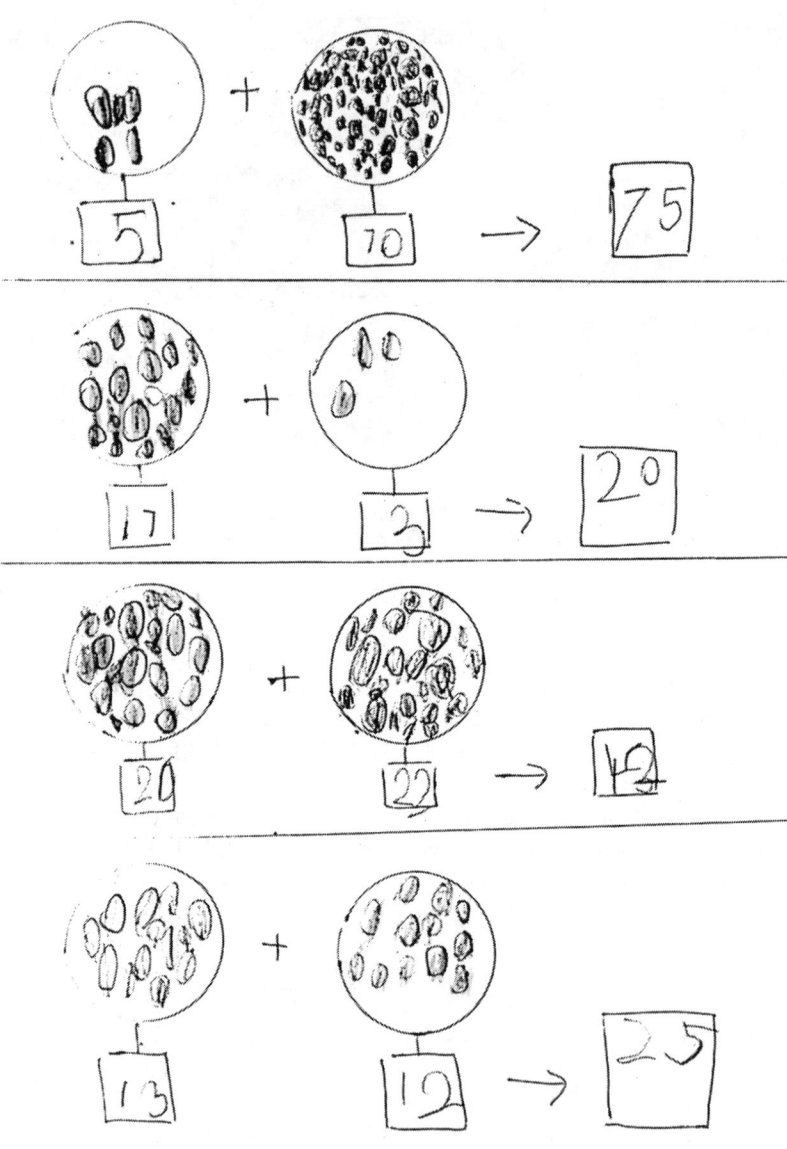

Figure 11.9 Sam's completed sheet

Note: On diagrams 5, 17, 3 20 and 12 all shading is blue.

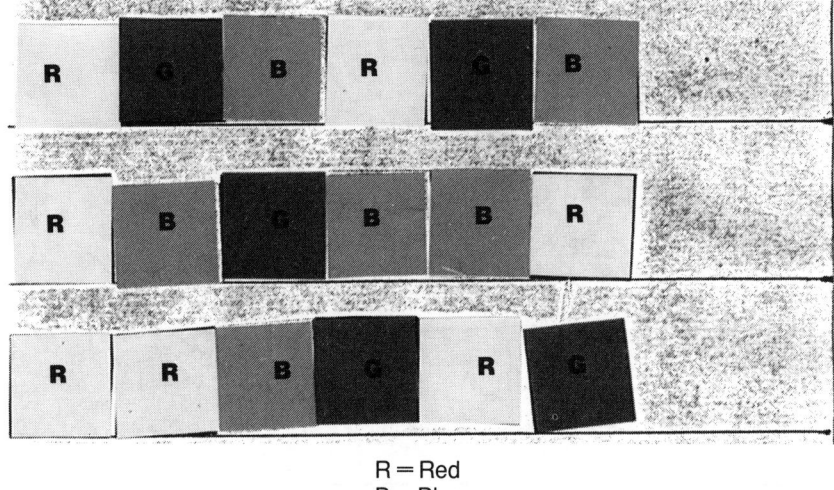

R = Red
B = Blue
G = Green

Figure 11.10 Carlly's patterning

became so sophisticated that we could talk of the children being involved in the sorts of processes discussed earlier (pp. 92–108), namely defining structures and developing them. The continuation of Carlly's work in figure 11.11 illustrates this.

I am continually on the look out for instances, such as the above, where some feature of a child's work could be brought out and developed. Further instances can be examined in the case-studies. To cite just one of many possible examples here, consider chapter 4, p. 34 where comments to Hayley (4.10) encouraged her to focus on and extend the patterning in her six by six squares.

Let us focus a little more sharply on the interaction between the children and the teacher in such cases. A child is working at something. The teacher sees within this the germ of an idea and somehow focuses attention on it. The child might already have been aware of it and might even have *intended* it to feature; in which case the teacher is merely serving to bring the idea out into the open and is, implicitly, showing approval of it. On the other hand, the teacher might be involving the child in framing a perception of it for the first time, or altering the child's original perception. The teacher plays a leading part here then, but there is a crucial difference between this and the usual 'passing on of ideas' role, for the emphasis is on what the child is actually doing, not just what the teacher knows about already.

There does not even have to be an explicit comment like 'I can see a pattern in what you are doing' followed by 'Now I'd like everyone to make a

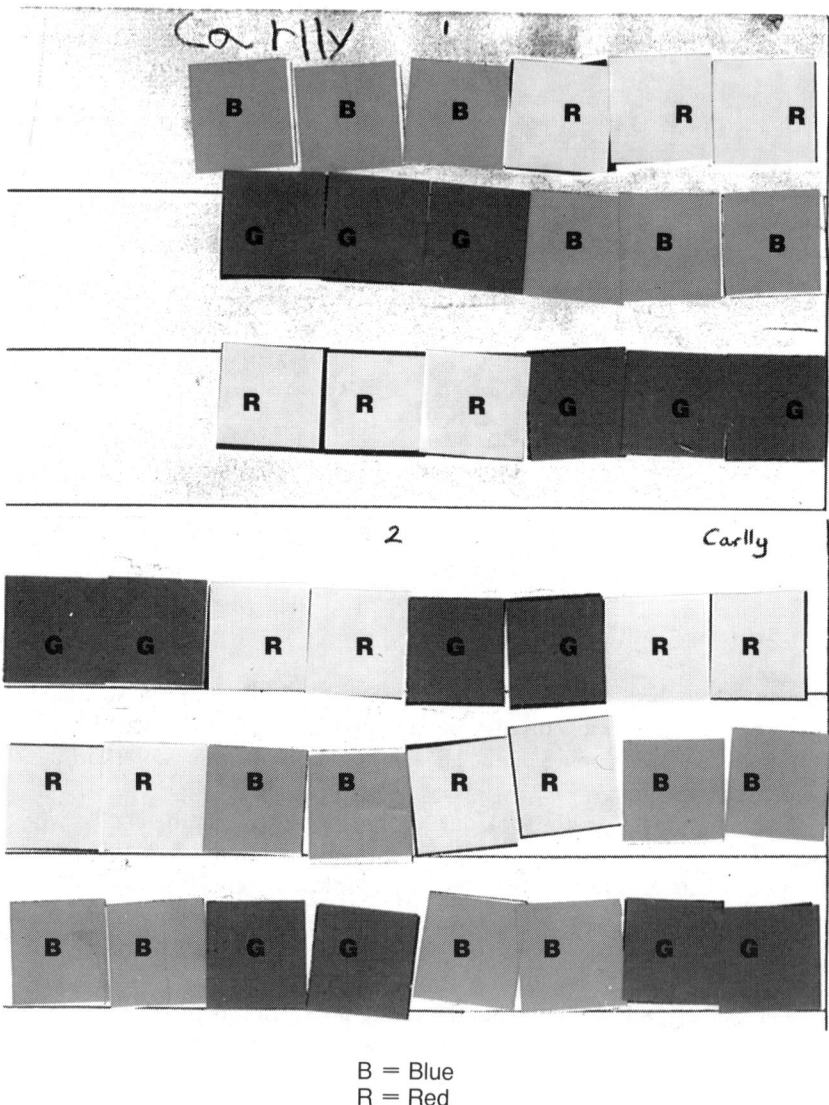

B = Blue
R = Red
G = Green

Figure 11.11 Showing the continuation of Carlly's work

pattern please.' One can often underplay the role even more than that. Indeed, in the cards example, I merely asked the children to talk about what they had done – the mention of 'pattern' came first from them.

There is frequently so much which can be developed from a mathematical point of view, even if this is not immediately obvious. For example, in the

'Six by six squares' activity, Alan's (4.11) 'mats' might seem disappointing at first, especially when they are compared with the other children's ideas. There is plenty to be developed here, however. Inviting Alan or other children to talk about what he has done might lead to a focus on such items as:

- counting the numbers of red, green and yellow squares;
- comparing the numbers of red, green or yellow squares on both mats;
- seeing which colour was used the most or the least;
- finding out on which mat he left the most space;
- seeing how many sets of, say, two adjoining squares have been coloured and deciding what is to count as such a case, etc.

Try reconsidering a piece of work which you feel at first is disappointing. Is there any potential for development?

Spontaneity

Often, without any direct invitation from the teacher, children put forward their own ideas in any case. If one of the main intentions is that children will participate in steering what happens in sessions, then any willingness to suggest ideas should be encouraged. Use can often be made of them immediately but, for various reasons, this is not always the case. For example, a group of children were seeing how many different sticks of two cubes they could make using just red and yellow as colours. Suddenly, Rachel (5.00) thought of using three cubes instead of two and held up an example of a stick.

At the time, I did not think the children had taken the two cubes situation as far as they might, for example we had not started on any debate as to whether they could be certain they had found all the two cubes sticks. So I did not really want the group, or even just Rachel, to start thinking about using sets of three cubes just then.

Could we make a list of the alternatives for action in such a situation?

In the above situation I commented on Rachel having a different idea and said that we could certainly try it in a minute, but suggested that for the moment we should concentrate on just using two cubes.

It seems important to show one's support for a spontaneously suggested idea even (especially?) if one is not going to encourage the children to concentrate on it at that moment. To make a remark such as 'But we're thinking about only two cubes at the moment' could be very discouraging and, once discouraged in one context, children might feel less like putting forward their own ideas in others, even if explicitly asked for them.

Often ideas *can* be taken up later. The three cubes suggestion does, of course, provide a natural extension to the two cubes work in any case. When encouraging children to start up such ideas later, I try to remember to make an explicit reference back to the original suggestion, for instance, 'Do you remember when Rachel had the idea of using three cubes? Let's have a go at that now.' I think this can help underline the fact that I *am* encouraging the children to come up with their own ideas.

Children often come up with more ideas than there is time to concentrate on. Inviting them to choose what to pursue seems sensible here. Choosing between alternatives plays a vital role in decision-making.

Children often do something spontaneously which, in my planning of the session, I had thought I might need to introduce myself. For example, in the 'Number squares' activity, Anne-Marie (5.08) made her squares into a three by three arrangement before I showed the children the three by three grids and invited them to put their squares in it (p. 45). Where possible, I think we should try not to make it obvious that we have already thought of the particular idea, but continue as if it were the child's idea only: 'Let's all have a go at what X has just done' etc. (cf. p. 135). The three by three squares incident was an exception, however, in that my pre-planning became evident when I produced the three by three grids. Having materials already prepared does potentially carry with it the disadvantage of detracting from a child's spontaneous initiative and perhaps conveys a feeling of 'we're supposed to be following this track then in any case'. In such circumstances, maybe we should stop and think whether we could do without the materials? It could, of course, take some courage *not* to bring out sheets etc., which have been time-consuming to prepare!

I sometimes fight quite hard to stop myself asking a question or suggesting an idea, to see if children might come up with it themselves. For example, when Hayley (4.10) started to produce the set of configurations on her six by six squares shown as figure 4.15 it was very tempting to ask her to find how many there were altogether!

Language

Another way in which one can show support for children's thinking is to take note of how individuals use or make up words to talk about what they are doing, then adopt the language oneself. For example, I showed a group of children a picture made of gummed shapes as represented in figure 11.12. They decided that the shapes looked like houses and set about making their own pictures of such houses. Most of them kept to using just one square with each triangle, but a few did not. This included Sam (4.11) who said that some of his shapes were 'flats' (see figure 11.13). When subsequently talking with the children about their pictures I then referred to 'flats' myself. Partly as a result of my questioning, the children became involved in deciding such things as what made a shape 'flats'; whether they would count figure 11.14 as 'flats' too, for example.

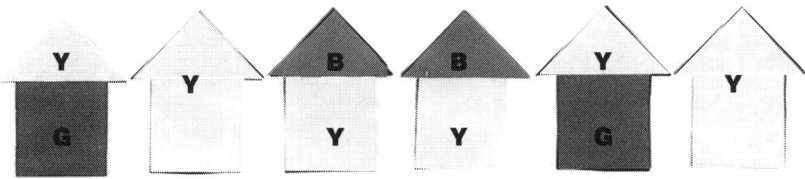

Figure 11.12 I showed the children a picture made of gummed shapes arranged thus

Y = Yellow
B = Blue
G = Green

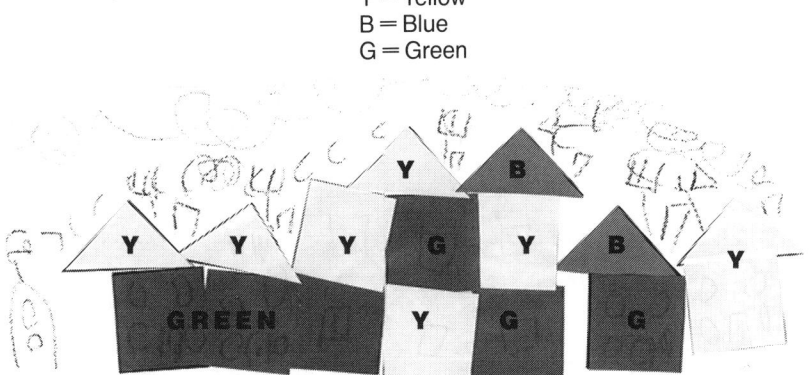

Figure 11.13 Sam's 'flats'

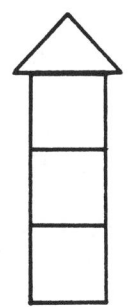

Figure 11.14 I discussed whether these could also be considered 'flats'

Sam's observation about 'flats' could have passed by without further comment, but here was an opportunity for it to act as a term whose usage becomes more closely defined. Making definitions is a vital constituent of mathematics and there seemed some parallels here.

Sometimes non-standard words might acquire a special shared meaning too. For example, Cirwyn (5.03) was colouring in as many different two by

147

two squares as she could, with two squares purple and two squares orange. Referring to a square which she had coloured like that in figure 11.15. I asked her to 'Tell me something about that one.' She said, 'That goes boing, boing, boing, boing', with the 'boings' pointing in turn firstly to the two purple squares, then to the two orange squares as in the diagram in figure 11.16.

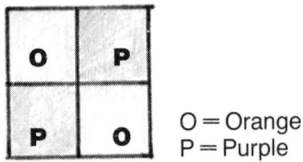

O = Orange
P = Purple

Figure 11.15 Cirwyn's coloured squares

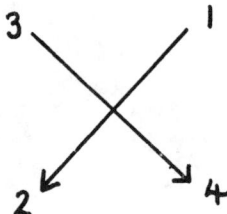

Figure 11.16 Showing how Cirwyn identified her pattern

I said, 'Let's think about the purple boing. Could you do the purple boing so it looks a bit different on another one? Does your purple boing have to be like that?'

It seems that, originally, Cirwyn's use of 'boing' simply accompanied her action of pointing out the diagonals, but my comment turned the use of the word into a noun, giving a name to the occurrence of two diagonal squares. It served to give us a name which marked out a feature which Cirwyn had perceived and this feature became an object for investigation. Implicitly, it also gave support to the making up of language.

What of the introduction of conventional terms? I can imagine readers now worried with thoughts like 'Cirwyn should really be learning to use words like "diagonal".' It seems important to remember, however, that it is often very hard to communicate one's thinking and this can be particularly the case for young children. If children acquire the feeling that they must *only* use 'proper' terms, then this could inhibit them from having a go at all. Any introduction of standard terms should thus be carried out sensitively, preferably after a need for them has been understood.

When looking at Cirwyn's work with the rest of the group later on, I actually mentioned to the children that they might hear some people talking about the purple squares being on a 'diagonal'. Also, at the start of another activity on a later occasion, I asked the children to colour in the little squares on the diagonals of larger squares of different sizes as illustrated in figure 11.17.

Figure 11.17 Colouring squares on diagonals

I referred back to the diagonals being what Cirwyn had called 'boings'. In both these instances the children were not put under the pressure of feeling that 'diagonal' was the only term they should be using.

Often, some children in a group will have prior knowledge of such conventional terms in any case and may well use them in other children's hearing. The teacher could seize upon this, saying such things as 'What do you think X means by "diagonal"?' Here, again, the emphasis is on X using the language and not on the teacher imposing it.

Some readers might feel that I am saying, 'Never tell children anything!' This is not what I am claiming. I am trying to emphasise the fact that premature introduction of a term before children know what they are talking about can be dangerous. The sudden arrival of a technical word needs to have coupled with it opportunities for exploration. These remarks about the use of words apply equally well to the use of other sorts of symbols.

Think of some conventional terms with which you want children to become familiar. Can you foresee any ways of enabling the children to become familiar with the notions before *the new terms are introduced?*

SOME THOUGHTS ON THE TEACHER'S AUTHORITY

Putting an emphasis on children participating in steering the direction of activities necessarily entails a lessening of emphasis on the teacher taking the lead. But the teacher is still the teacher, and the children are still the children and there are all sorts of explicit and implicit facets to these roles which continually help set the scene and frame what happens. As examples:

- children may be encouraged to suggest their own ideas, but I am doing the encouraging;
- I call the children by their first names but they call me 'Miss Bird';
- I praise the children but they do not praise me;

149

- if I ask the children to do something, I (and they) expect it to be done;
- I announce things to everybody, but the children do not normally do so unless invited.

Can you add to this list?

It would be difficult to imagine some of the usual features of the pupil/ teacher roles being changed, but much of the discussion in the earlier sections of this chapter points to my trying to *underplay* my own role. There are still some further issues to be developed, particularly in connection with the notion of the teacher's authority.

For our purposes, 'authority' is used in at least two different senses.[6] One of these is where we would talk about a person being an authority on something, implying that they have greater knowledge than some others in this area. This is what is often meant by the word 'expertise'. I shall refer to it as 'sense 1'. The other is intimately tied up with notions such as discipline, obedience and power. I shall refer to this as 'sense 2'.

Authority in sense 1 (as the expert)

I believe that most teachers expect to be used as a resource in the classroom. They expect children to ask things like 'How do you write "fourteen"?' when they need to know. Sometimes we might not answer such things directly but point children in the direction of trying to find out for themselves, as when a number ladder was offered to Ben (5.05) to help him work out how to write the numerals for twelve (p. 50). For me this is likely to be because I see a way of freeing children from having to rely on me on other occasions. Sometimes, however, I might well give an immediate response. This is particularly likely if it seems that to do otherwise would detract unhelpfully from the rest of the activity.

When faced with children doing something incorrectly I find I often fight back the temptation to correct them, and wait instead to see if they sort this out themselves. For example, when Jemma (5.04) wrote 'p' instead of '9' (figure 3.16), I did not comment. Then, on a later occasion, the children found that reading 'There are "p" sets of two dots' did not make sense. Ilona (5.04) suggested that 'p' should be a number and Sam (5.03) explained that the 'p' was the wrong way round (see p. 31). Here, then, the children certainly did correct Jemma's mistake themselves. Moreover, it was implicit in this episode that there are reasons for writing something a particular way round, otherwise it might lead to confusion. The children have appreciated such confusion for themselves without the teacher needing to comment. Otherwise, my authority in terms of 'knowing how to write something' could easily have been confused with authority in terms of 'you must simply do as you are told'.

In what other ways and in what situations do you think the two senses of 'authority' might become confused?

Instead of just waiting to see if children sort out something themselves, other children can be asked explicitly what *they* think. This was the case when Sam (5.04) claimed that nine and ten gave eighteen (p. 72). Instead of ignoring this, or counting along with Sam, it was brought out into the open by saying 'Shall we have a look at that, then? Sam makes it different, he doesn't make it nineteen, he makes it eighteen.' Bringing something out into the open like this can lead to arguments amongst the children. We may be wary of provoking such, but surely they can be a constructive means of children sorting something out themselves? Some related points will be discussed later.

Sometimes, again without making any comments at the time, a child's apparent misconception is stored away as something to be worked on later, perhaps during another session. For example, when Daniel (5.06) appeared to accept only equilateral triangles as triangles (p. 59), a mental note was made to involve the group in some activities with miscellaneous sorts of triangles on another occasion.

When returning to the area, there is no need to mention any previous possible misconceptions. The idea can be treated anew. Perhaps Daniel's group could work on an activity such as making some three-sided shapes on a nine-pin geoboard. Some of the children might refer to these shapes as triangles; or there might be a debate about which are triangles and which are not, or one might comment that we could call all of the shapes 'triangles', etc. Whatever happens, there is likely to be plenty of opportunity for the use of the word 'triangle' to be clarified (and there is further potential in this activity too, of course).

If it is obvious in a session that children *do* realise that they have made a mistake, this can often still be used positively. For example, as described in chapter 3, Sam (5.03) counted ten circles in a rectangle on the circles sheet, but Jemma (5.04) and Matthew (5.05) made it nine and Matthew said it was Sam who was wrong, which it was. Sam recounted and made it nine (p. 19). Saying something like 'So you *were* wrong before' would not have been helpful in any way, but asking 'What do you think happened when you made it ten?' involved Sam in some further thinking and, indeed, his 'one more' answer gave some further insight into his capabilities.

Are there other issues that ought to be explored in connection with the fact that I want to introduce children to culturally determined conventions (symbols, terms, etc.) and encourage them to use them correctly, whilst all the time also seeking to underplay my role?

Authority in sense 2 (as the person in charge)

Often we may want children to behave differently from the way they are behaving at that moment. We may want them to make less noise, be more tidy, pay more attention, be more careful, and so on. We may frequently find ourselves commenting directly on such matters ('Keep the noise down please!' etc.) but might there not sometimes be some alternatives, more in keeping with the spirit of trying to underplay one's role?

Let us consider an example. Leanne (5.04) was trying to see how many coloured spots there were altogether on a set of cards. This was a daunting task which she had set herself: there were in fact forty spots to be counted! Others in the group were talking quite loudly while Leanne was counting. Suddenly she announced that she could not think because of the noise. I stopped the rest of the children and asked Leanne to repeat what she had said. The other children then quietened down.

One possibility, then, is to use children's own perceptions of there being too much noise etc. Also, such incidents can always be referred to again later, especially with young children: 'Do you remember what Leanne said about not being able to think? Perhaps it's too noisy again now.'

Other forms of indirect control are, of course, commonly used and perhaps seem obvious but they warrant a short mention in this context because of their ability to focus attention away from the teacher's authoritarian role. Of particular note is that we can often stop children doing something by simply focusing their attention on something else rather than making an issue over stipulating that they must not do the first thing. For example, as can be seen in the transcript in chapter 8, at one point when Joseph (4.10), Leanne (5.00) and Xanthe (4.10) were engaged in discussing the stick of cubes, Cirwyn (5.00) suddenly pulled at her cardigan and said, 'My Nanny knitted this!' I remarked 'Did she, Cirwyn?' to which she continued, 'My Nan knits a lot of things.' (p. 79) How off-putting it could have been to have told Cirwyn that she should be thinking about the cubes and not her jumper! Was it not perfectly reasonable for her to tell us proudly about it? Yet I wanted her to re-engage in the activity. This was effected by asking her a direct question: 'Cirwyn, could you, Cirwyn, come here and tell us anything else about this?'

When we *do* overtly stop children from doing things, or tell them what they must do, perhaps we can strive as far as possible to give reasons for the restrictions? Letting children in on some of our own decision-making could mean that we are appealing more to their sense than to our authority. So when rejecting the idea of glueing the papers on the classroom wall (p. 28), an explanation was given that the class teacher might not be very pleased if they were on there forever.

And before making some adverse comment about something, perhaps we should stop and ask ourselves whether it might actually have been a reasonable interpretation of the task in any case? An example might help to clarify what I mean here. Lisa's (5.00) colouring of her six by six squares was disappointing as she had not kept to the squares and I could not immediately see anything much of a mathematical nature which could be gleaned from it through discussion (p. 34). But, in inviting the children to colour in the papers originally, nothing was said about keeping to the squares so there was no reason to have expected Lisa to have done so. (See p. 137 for a discussion of a similar example from chapter 7.)

Do you have any examples of your own?

To imply that children should have acted differently when, in fact, what they did was perfectly reasonable could discourage them unfairly and perhaps even inhibit them when they are starting to engage in activities on other occasions. It is all too easy to encourage children to slip into a 'got to guess what is in the teacher's mind' attitude.

In analysing what has been said to children, I find that the most evocative form is not to explicitly *tell* them to do something but more to *invite* them to do it. As examples: 'Would you like to see, Joseph?' (p. 75), 'Could we, perhaps, put these back together again now we've dismantled them?' (p. 79).

On the surface, using this particular mode of engaging children in activities might seem insignificant and perhaps sometimes it is. The children might not perceive that they have any choice in the matter ... and I am not sure I always intend them to have in any case. I think, however, that it is fair to say that often when I use phrases such as these I do so with the possibility in mind that the children could reject the idea for something else. (NB. The 'something else' is important – I cannot imagine being content with a straightforward 'No!' in situations like this.) Trying to give children space to make their own suggestions becomes part and parcel of the way one acts and it seeps into the way of phrasing what some might state as direct instructions. Even if children interpret that I really do want them to do what I am phrasing as an invitation, they might still somehow sense that their agreement is important!

What else could I have said instead of, say, 'Could we, perhaps, put these back together again now we've dismantled them?' How about, 'Now put them back together, please.' They would *have* to do this now. Might not this definite instruction imply that I had something else definite in mind too, for example a particular way of assembling the blocks? Perhaps the children might have felt that I was expecting the cubes to be put in the same order as before and would not have risked trying anything different? Children sometimes seem to imagine that there are constraints on activities when the teacher has not actually intended such. Perhaps trying to phrase something as a suggestion rather than as an instruction can help in the fostering of an atmosphere in which children feel that it is acceptable to participate in structuring what happens?

Do you have any examples of your own in which children imagined that there were constraints on activities which you had not intended? Can we do anything about this?

Another usual facet of a teacher's role, and one which is implicit in much of what I have said before, is that of praising children. On the surface it might seem that praising children can only be positive, but there is more to be said, particularly in the light of the fact that we are discussing encouraging children to take their own initiatives.

Praise of one child can make others feel that what they are doing is valued less. Consider Xanthe's comment at the end of the 'A stick of cubes' episode, now reprinted here:

Joseph (4.10): I thought of a good way, didn't I?
MB: You did.
Xanthe (4.10): Next time, I'm going to thought [*sic*] of a good way.

Joseph's question put pressure on me to respond although I had not intended to mark out what he had done with particular praise, especially as he had a tendency to dominate activities in any case. My reply 'You did' simply agreed with him, not elaborating the praiseworthy element of it any further. Even this short sequence, however, seems to have led to Xanthe feeling that what she had so far was not as valued as what Joseph had done.

Even choosing to follow up one child's idea rather than somebody else's (for example, involving the rest of the group in Hayley's (4.10) idea for the six by six squares, see p. 41) serves as indirect praise of what that child has done. What do the others feel about this? Perhaps we need to try to ensure that everyone's ideas somehow feature in a similar way in turn?

Praising children, of course, also serves to emphasise teacher control – the *teacher* is valuing something. Children might do something to obtain the teacher's praise instead of doing so for reasons more intrinsic to the activity.

Having said all this, however, I am not going to argue for not praising children at all. Even if I wished to, I doubt that I could stop an immediate and human response to interesting features of what I perceive children to be doing.

Of course, children might interpret a lack of praise negatively in any case and thus be discouraged from putting forward and pursuing ideas. Most children are used to looking to their parents and other adults for encouragement and to deny such might make them feel very insecure.

Some research has suggested that teacher acknowledgement of what a child has done, in terms of telling him that he has done well etc., acts differently from the giving of extrinsic material rewards (stars, team-points etc.) in any case. It would seem that the giving of the latter for the successful completion of an activity can actually make the activity itself *less* appealing later whereas verbal encouragement can have the opposite effect.[7]

However, I am arguing the case for not blindly praising children as if this is always a good thing. I feel that praise should also be sincere. Children can be quick to detect the difference between praise for its own sake and genuine acknowledgement of something worthwhile. This links with the importance of children coming to trust their teacher (see the following section). Insincerity is hardly likely to help in the building up of trust.

PUTTING CHILDREN AT EASE

It seems most probable that the more children feel uncomfortable in a situation, the less prepared they will be to put their own ideas forward and pursue them. They are more likely to 'play safe', particularly if they are working under an umbrella of what they still perceive as the teacher-dominating activities. So we might well ask how we can avoid children feeling uncomfortable? On the other hand, there is bound to be an uncertain element in any learning and a degree of risk-taking is essential. How can the teacher support a child within this sense of insecurity associated with learning? There are no simple answers to these interrelated questions but the following discussion points to some of the facets of teaching which might have a bearing on these matters.

It seems very important that children should be able to develop trust in their teacher. This may seem obvious but it is all too easy, for example, to be inconsistent in the way one acts. For instance, suppose one had told some children that one wants them to put forward their own ideas about some-thing and a child then comes up with a suggestion which does not seem sensible to the teacher? It would be very easy to be immediately dismissive, but how might the child feel and how much less likely to make a suggestion on another occasion?

What other inconsistencies might arise?

Children frequently do come up with impractical ideas, however, so what can one do? Let them find out themselves that something is impractical? Ask other children what they think, in the hopes that someone else (that is, not you) will see the impracticality and lack of sense? These are certainly possibilities, but even so they might not cover all eventualities. For example it would not cover the instance discussed on page 152 where I did not want the children to follow up Matthew's (5.05) suggestion of gluing their rectangles of paper on to the classroom wall! If one is going to dismiss an idea oneself, perhaps it is important to do so with what we might think of as a 'light touch'. To reaffirm a point made in connection with the gluing example, actually putting the children in a position of seeing why the idea is best not taken up seems sensible. Then the children might appreciate the reasoning behind a rejection and not just be confronted with the rejection itself.

Mistakes

Mistakes are inevitable when one is learning and the teacher's reaction to these can be crucial (cf. p. 151). Children can so easily be made to feel silly and may well start to adopt defensive attitudes and want to hide what they are doing. It seems important that mistakes are treated with a 'what can we do about it?' approach or 'what can this tell us about what to do next?' stance. Consider the reaction and Jemma's (5.04) correction of six to four spots in this light (p. 22).

Much the same could be said about the showing of ignorance. If we want to be able to facilitate children's learning then we often need to make assessments of their current thinking. But involving children in situations where there is an emphasis on their displaying their own perceptions means that one will be continually faced with glimpses into what they do *not* know as well as what they *do* know. Our attitude here is important. It would be so easy to knock children's confidence by implying that they should already know something when, in fact, they appear not to.

For example, well into the 'A stick of cubes' activity, Cirwyn (5.00) exclaimed 'I know what: if you see that number' (looking at the '6' on the 'hat' I had in my hand) 'that means there's six of them blocks.' (p. 77) After the initial discussions, I had taken it for granted that all the children in the group had appreciated that this was what the number on the hat would normally mean, but it could have been very off-putting to Cirwyn had I expressed my surprise with such a remark as 'Hadn't you worked that out already?' or 'Goodness, have you only just thought of that?'

Assimilating ideas

Children need time to learn new ideas and relate them to previous understanding. If they are to be flexible in their thinking, they need to meet ideas in a variety of contexts, having opportunities to forge countless connections and review past notions anew. For various reasons, we might feel pressure upon us to rush children through activities but we need to remember that this could prove counter-productive in the long run. It may also help to keep reassuring ourselves that if children are working actively at mathematics, then they often seem to be linking together a whole web of ideas at once (cf. p. 88) and going a lot further than one would anticipate they might.

Meaningful settings

I have already mentioned the importance of the teacher involving young infants in situations which make human sense (cf. p. 100 and point (3), p. 124) but further mention of this seems appropriate here. Children are much more likely to feel at ease in meaningful contexts which are part-and-parcel of their world than in situations which appear more alien and over which they feel they have less control. (This is the 'embedded'/'disembedded' distinction of Donaldson's (1984) referred to on p. 100.) Given a meaningful setting, perhaps children might then feel secure enough to start to push beyond its bounds themselves? This is likely to be particularly the case if children are working within an atmosphere where the teacher is encouraging them to participate in steering what happens.

Sensitive responses

However much care we have taken in setting up a situation, we have all experienced numerous instances of seeing children looking anxious or otherwise distressed. What to us can seem to be a tiny, unimportant detail can appear overwhelmingly significant to a child and some sensitive handling may be necessary to try to stem the growing disquiet.

For example, when Sam (5.04) and Matthew (5.06) pointed out that Ilona (5.05) had written the numeral for 'two' in two different ways, this seemed to upset Ilona somewhat (p. 66). Imagine the effect of a teacher-type remark such as, 'Now you must try to remember to write it the correct way.' And how often, in an attempt to explain why something is incorrect, do we make what is in effect a ridiculous remark such as, 'Oh dear! We don't know what that means!' when of course it is obvious what was intended. Surely such a remark does not square with encouraging children to build up trust in what we say?

Can you think of other remarks which purport to give reasons but which actually do not?

The very fact that children are not working completely as individuals but can see and hear what others are doing can itself cause anxieties. X comments that she has finished something before Y; Z shows that he can do something which Y knows she cannot, etc. There is nothing unusual about this, it occurs frequently even if one is not working in a particularly open way with the children. But if one *is* encouraging the children's own ideas then other features emerge. In particular, one needs to watch that a particular child's ideas do not dominate, with the result that others feel that they cannot come up with good ideas. This links with the points about praise (page 154). One might encourage some children and play down the suggestions of others. Now it is these 'others' who might feel discouraged! Perhaps the rejection of ideas can itself be carried out in as supportive a way as possible?

I had this in mind when I said to Matthew (5.06) about not using his plate of biscuits sheet (p. 72). This was why I explained that we had used Matthew's and Sam's work on other occasions and so we would use Ilona's and Jemma's for a change. I also commented to Matthew that it was nothing to do with his sheet not being 'good' in any way, because it was.

Coping with difficulties

Children often show signs of anxiety when they find something difficult. As I shall argue later, this does not mean that we should try to remove all potential difficulties from a situation, far from it. However, one's attitude to something which could potentially be conceived as 'difficult' seems important and is worthy of some discussion here.

I often agree with children when they say, or appear to be implying, that something is difficult. Why? Because it might help set their minds at rest if part of their worry has hinged upon thinking that I *expect* them to cope easily. And I do not want children to feel that it is somehow wrong to find something difficult, as this might start to inhibit them from setting themselves challenges. Consider the alternatives. Suppose I say, 'Oh come along, that's really easy' or some other such remark. The easiness or difficulty of a task is relative to the person doing it: knowing that a teacher thinks of something as 'easy' is hardly going to help solve the child's own difficulty, indeed it is more likely simply to make him feel guilty about it.

When agreeing that something is difficult it seems important not to do so with a negative 'so you'll never do it' sort of attitude since that could in itself thwart the taking on of challenges. It could also imply that the teacher knows all about the idea in advance, thus going against intentions of striving to play down one's own knowledge and expectations.

So far, I have been talking of *agreeing* with children when they seem to find something difficult. Would I think it appropriate sometimes to announce in advance that I think something is difficult? My instant reaction is to deny the usefulness of this for similar reasons as those given above: it could tend to underline *my* thinking and 'easy' and 'difficult' can never be anything but subjective labels in any case. On the other hand, much depends on the way one expresses this expectation of difficulty. If serving to communicate a 'what a challenge but let's take it on' attitude it could prove positively helpful in engaging children in an activity in the first place.

For example, the question, 'How on earth do you think we could try and get nineteen doing what Jemma was doing? ...' (p. 21) implied a possible difficulty but in a challenging sort of way, which perhaps helped to heighten the children's satisfaction in finding a solution which worked.

How else can we strive to put children at ease? What do we do which actually acts against this?

INVOLVEMENT IN COMPLEXITY AND CONFLICTING IDEAS

All too readily coupled with the notion of 'putting children at ease' is the idea of smoothing things out for them, bypassing struggles, trying to avoid dilemmas arising and so on. I am not arguing for such. On the contrary, I believe much can be gained from children's involvement in situations where they have to grapple with complexity and conflicting ideas. Indeed, sometimes I involve children in such situations on purpose. I will start by considering an example of this.

In the 'A stick of cubes' activity, I began by showing children a stick of seven cubes with a '6' hat on it. The children's awareness of there being something not quite right sparked off quite a lengthy and often surprisingly involved debate concerning possible interpretations and what could be done to rectify the situation. Consider the depth of reasoning engaged in by the children in such parts of the discussion as:

Joseph: But if you put that on (*meaning the hat*) there'll be seven. If we take that off there'll be the right number.

Xanthe: But if we don't have that on we won't know which ... how many there is!

Surely this is quite staggering, particularly when we remember that these children were not yet five (cf. p. 101)?

Hence it can be seen that involving children in situations where they perceive an inconsistency or mistake has the potential for capturing their interest. Trying to sort out inconsistencies can prove to be compelling.

What other inconsistent situations might we offer to children for their interpretation and development?

I can now imagine some readers thinking such things as 'Surely we shouldn't show children something which is wrong?' Such anxieties, however, are intimately tied up with a conception of teaching as the passing on of facts. If we are prepared to relax this so that our emphasis is more on encouraging children to make and discuss their own interpretations of situations, then we need not have such worries. (And, in any case, it is clear from the 'A stick of cubes' transcript that no one has gone away with the idea that '6' is the label one must always associate with seven cubes.)

Arriving at different answers is something else which can attract children's attention as a matter to be resolved. This often occurs naturally within the course of events. For example, see chapter 3, p. 30 where Ilona (5.04) and Jemma (5.04) were actually counting two different things. If we want to make the most of these occurrences it seems important not to resolve the situation ourselves ('Let's all count together' etc.) but to bring out the differences and hence, implicitly or explicitly, invite some solution.

We might even actively encourage the occurrence of such situations. One way of striving for this would be to use language ambiguously on purpose. For example, I might ask 'How many shapes are there?' where I realise that 'shapes' could be interpreted in different ways by different children.

Here is such a situation in action: Lianne had made the two strips of 'houses' shown as (a) and (b) in figure 11.18. She and five other children were engaged in comparing them. They had made various comparisons

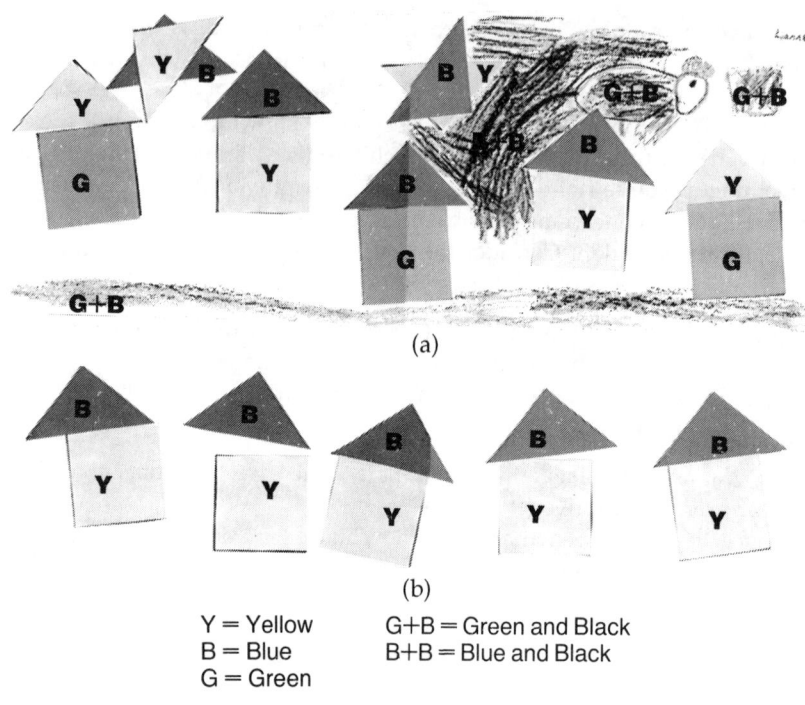

Y = Yellow   G+B = Green and Black
B = Blue   B+B = Blue and Black
G = Green

Figure 11.18 Lianne's strips of 'houses'

themselves when I asked which strip had more shapes on it. This sparked off the following sequence:

Hayley (4.10): I counted them.
Lianne (5.03): That one's got more. (*a*)
MB: You counted them, did you Hayley? What did you find out?
Lianne: That one's got ... that one's got more. (*a*)
Hayley: That they've both got the same.
MB: They've both got the same. You (*to Hayley*) think they've both got the same, but you (*to Lianne*) don't?
Lianne: 'Cos there's one, two, three, four, five, six, seven, eight, nine, *ten*; (*counting along* (b)) and one, two, three four, five, six, seven, eight, nine, ten, eleven, twelve, thirteen, *fourteen*. (*counting along* (a))
Hayley: They've both got five on! One, two, three, four, *five*. One, two, three, four, *five* (*counting along* (a) *and* (b) *in turn*). They've both got five! They've both got five on! Look: one, two, three, four, *five*!
Lianne: Fourteen!

160

MB: (*To the rest of the group as well as Lianne and Hayley*) Now listen to this! This is a bit strange I think! Because you're (Lianne) saying there's fourteen things on this one ...

Lianne: 'Cos I'm counting the roofs.

MB: 'Cos you're counting the roofs. But what are *you* saying, Hayley?

Hayley: There's five on each one.

MB: You're saying there's five on each one. So why have we got different answers? Why are the girls getting different answers?

Alan (4.11):   (*Pointing to a shape like that in figure 11.19 and presumably meaning the whole of it.*) Because Hayley's counting *them* but Lianne's counting the house and the roof.

Hayley: That's one house, that's one house, that's one house ... (*pointing to three shapes as in figure 11.19 in turn.*)

MB: So Lianne is counting all the different shapes isn't she? All these little shapes (*pointing to a square and a triangle separately*) that make up the big shapes. But Hayley is counting these together. So you're both right!

Another feature to be pointed out in this extract is that I have focused on the fact that both children are right at once. See chapter 8, p. 77, for a further example of this too. What is 'correct' in mathematics is not correct *in vacuo* but depends on the context and decisions which have been made. To think that young children can only cope with 'simple' situations in which there is one right answer is not only false but could also give a wrong slant to children's developing ideas about the nature of mathematics.

In the above example, the word 'shape' was purposefully introduced in an ambiguous way. Without such a move on my part, I have found that situations often evolve where children are using words differently. For example, in the six by six squares activity, when discussing the shape shown in figure 11.20, configurations which Hayley had devised, some children talked of the tiny square being the 'middle' one. Others, however, talked of the square outside this (but inside the largest square) as being the 'middle' one (pp. 41–4).

Figure 11.19 Alan pointed out the difference between counting the whole shape and counting the 'house' and 'roof' separately

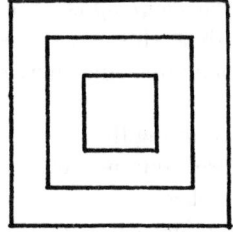

Figure 11.20 The basic squared paper used in the six by six squares activity

Whilst actually carrying out the activity themselves and talking about it beforehand, none of the children seemed to have any difficulties with this double use of 'middle'; indeed, they might not have been aware of it. On a later occasion, however, when the group were talking with some other children about what they had been doing, some confusion did arise. It proved a good tactic to invite the children to think of something else to call one of the regions so that we could tell the two apart. Adam (5.03) suggested that the innermost square could be referred to as the 'very middle' and this was adopted whilst keeping 'middle' for the other region.

Some teachers might be worried about the idea of letting, or even encouraging, confusions to arise. But if we always try to avoid confusions occurring or to smooth them out ourselves when they do, how will children ever learn to tackle this themselves? Involvement in confusion can be a positive thing in that one can gain from engaging in trying to sort it out. Often, as in the example just discussed, the sorting out can lead to an appreciation of the necessity for making a definition, and defining is a process which has a significant role to play in mathematics.

It seems important to create positive approval for eagerness of the 'let me sort it out' kind. Young children frequently display such an attitude but they often learn not to bother – an adult will tell you the answer if you ask them!

There are other sorts of occasions when I try to stop myself from smoothing things out. One of these is when something is not going to work, or at least not going to work in the way envisaged. To refrain from commenting encourages the children to find this out for themselves. For example, when another group of children were working with the sheets of circles discussed in chapter 3, Rachel (5.02) suggested colouring in *nine* circles on each of the sets of circles! I let her begin! She was highly amused when she realised that every set would be completely filled in and look the same.

A similar sort of occasion is when I see that something is impossible. For example, when Cirwyn (5.01) and Joseph (4.11) were trying to make different-length strips of squares by putting strips five squares long and strips four squares long end to end (cf. p. 94), they spent a long time trying to make a strip eleven squares long. Why refrain from intervening here?

Because such situations have potential for children asking themselves such questions as:

- 'Is there no way to be found?'
- 'Why doesn't it work?'
- 'What makes it different?'
- 'How can I alter what I started with?'
- 'How can I change the rules so that it *does* work?'

Subsequently, through their own volition, children might become involved in trying to follow up such questions.

Of course, children might sometimes feel disheartened when they find that something is impossible. Here it seems important to point out that it is often just as important to find that something does *not* work, as it is to find a solution for something else. In a sense it is a positive thing to discover that something cannot be done, and an important part of mathematics.

How can we communicate this to children?

In fact, in the example just considered, Cirwyn and Joseph did not seem disheartened at all. Indeed, Joseph eventually came up with an amusing alternative. Having lined up two four square strips and one five square strip and found that that was too long, he announced that he could cut two squares of the five strip to give him a three strip, then he would be able to make an eleven strip! He also went on to think about which other strips he could make if he acquired a three strip.

Is it better not to interfere when children suggest something which is likely to present some problems? For example, as already remarked on (p. 135), when Matthew (5.05) suggested counting *all* the circles on his sheet it seemed he might not be entirely able to cope with this, but I did refrain from stopping him.

Think how Matthew might have felt had his idea been discouraged. Moreover, it is the very involvement in things with which we are not already secure which can give rise to seeing a need for and engaging in further learning. Wanting to count all the circles led to Matthew needing the words for 'fifty', 'sixty', 'seventy' and 'eighty' and being involved in some mention of the fact that it would not be sensible to use the same number word twice when counting (cf. p. 114). This is altogether different from a teacher announcing 'Today we are going to learn some more words for counting in tens', where the emphasis would be on what the teacher wants the children to learn, rather than on what they themselves see a need for learning. Indeed, I sometimes purposefully involve children in an activity which I think is going to give rise to some difficulties so that they can see a need for doing/learning something else. A great deal of sensitivity is needed in recognising when this is a manageable situation and not something quite out of control. Again it has to be said that eventually the children need to be able to recognise problems beyond their, or even our, present skills and not be upset by it.

There is something psychologically rather different in situations in which children encounter something with which they cannot cope and actually leave it, and those when a teacher has set the task in the first place. If a teacher sets a task, this carries with it the expectation that the teacher thinks you should be able to do it. If you cannot, not only have you not coped with the task, you have also 'failed' in the sense of not meeting the teacher's expectations. To not succeed at your *own* choice of task does not carry with it the same sort of pressure. And a sensitive teacher might sow some seeds for returning to the problem another day. Remembering such could give some motivation for introducing an item on a later occasion. ('Do you remember when some of you got stuck trying to do _____. Let's have a look at this again now.')

Sometimes children come up with ideas which it seems will take a long time to complete. I may have various niggling thoughts at the back of my mind about this: Will the children tire of the idea? Perhaps they will not be able to exhaust it? How 'useful' in terms of covering the syllabus is such a prolonged activity likely to prove? But letting the children go ahead can often be very fruitful:

- The very fact that the idea is the children's own may serve to sustain their interest for a surprising length of time.
- Perhaps not exhausting something does not matter? There may even be opportunities for thinking ahead: 'Well, you know you haven't found all the ways yet, but have you any idea about how many more there will be?' etc.
- I am often staggered by how much of the syllabus has been encountered when I analyse children's activities afterwards (cf. p. 88).
- Sometimes if children come to appreciate the enormity of a task they have set themselves, they make their own decisions about restricting it in some way.

As an example, consider the following. Having seen how many different sticks could be made from putting together just two cubes from a pile of red and yellow ones (cf. p. 145), Sam (5.00) suggested using *five* cubes. There would be many possibilities here, but he was encouraged to go ahead. Certainly Sam did not find all the possible combinations but many other items arose. As examples he made the sticks illustrated in figure 11.21 one after the other and said that they were different. When asked how they were also the same, he commented on 'a one-pattern'. He went on to make another pair of sticks which were the opposites of one another in terms of the red and yellow being interchanged (see figure 11.22). Other children perceived what he was doing and were able to make up further pairs themselves.

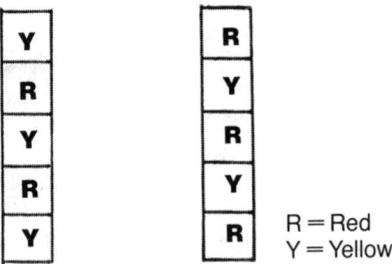

Figure 11.21 Sam's first pair of sticks

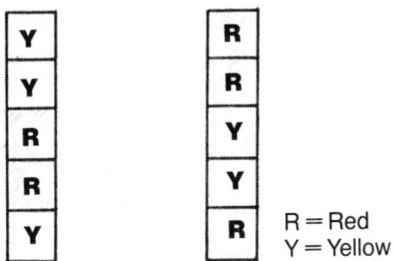

Figure 11.22 Sam's second pair of sticks

Jemma (5.01) thought of recording the sticks on paper so that each child could remember his/hers the following week. Sam chose to record his sticks on squared paper, using a square for each cube (see figure 11.23). Rachel (5.00) had the idea of swapping the papers so that everyone could try to make up someone else's. This they did the following week. Jemma worked from Sam's sheet and there was a lot of discussion about whether what she had made up from it was what Sam had intended. Throughout the sessions there was much counting and comparing of the sticks which had been made so far.

So Sam's suggestion gave rise to sustained involvement in a whole variety of activities, covering a range of processes and items of content from the syllabus.

Different conceptions

The children with whom one works will have a whole host of different conceptions and attitudes. No two children will think about something in exactly the same way because our conceptions are inextricably bound up with what we have done before, and each child's intricate web of past experiences will be unique. This in itself means that one is put it a position of great complexity. It can be misleading to talk of 'What everyone knows to

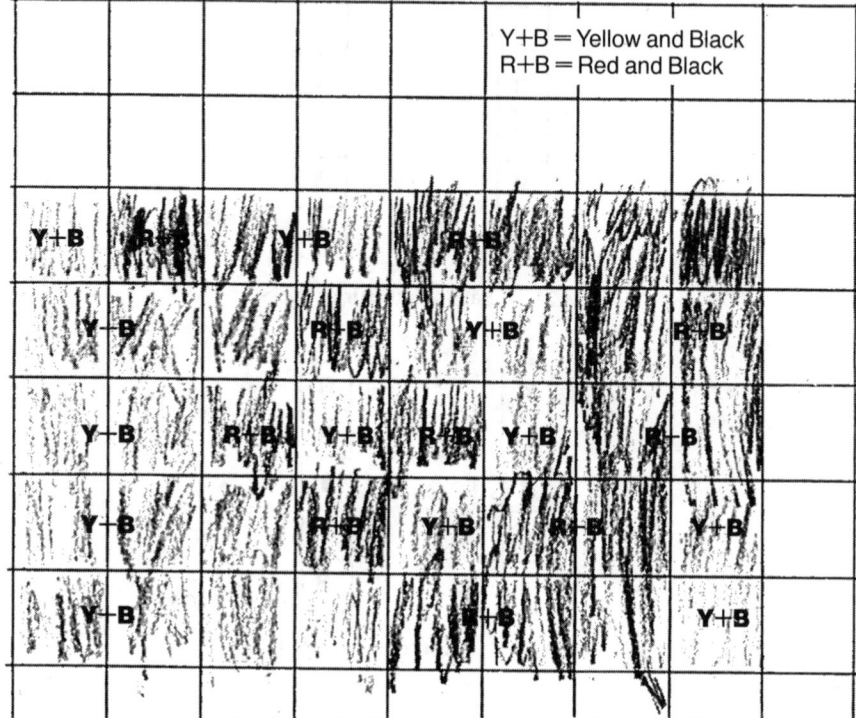

Y+B = Yellow and Black
R+B = Red and Black

Figure 11.23 Sam's record of his sticks

date', 'Where they have got to', etc. And not only is this because of differences amongst the children, but also because of the fact that there may only be a very rough correspondence between what we think children understand and what they do actually understand. We need to recognise the diversity and act accordingly, trying to create situations where the emphasis is on children pushing forward their own thinking, giving us glimpses into what this might be.

Ironically, what we often do with the best of intentions proves to be counter-productive. For example, we might think it helpful to break up what we see as a complex task into a series of easy to manage steps; the writing of recipe-type workcards falls into this category. But the children are now constrained to follow our pathway and, in so doing, may miss the underlying purpose of the task. Furthermore, many teachers think it is important to close a lesson by summing up what has happened. Sometimes this can be helpful but how often does the view we put on an activity not square with the children's? And again, what of the jaggedness of the different children's thinking?

Consider this example: Cirwyn (5.04), Leanne (5.04), Joseph (5.02) and Xanthe (5.02) were working with some cards which had coloured spots on either side of them (cf. p. 152). At Leanne's suggestion, each became involved in trying to see how many spots there were altogether. Counting and recounting gave rise to a series of different answers: 41, 32, 37, 40. Suddenly, much to my amazement, Joseph had the insight that the 'right proper answer', as he called it, must be forty. He knew that the children had ten spots each on the cards in front of them and claimed 'Ten, ten, ten and ten: that makes forty ... four people have got ten ... twenty and twenty makes forty'! It was very tempting to close the episode by confirming that forty must be the answer, then. Instead, I asked the others what they thought about Joseph's thinking and this did indeed reveal that they were not certain that it was all right. In retrospect I was glad to have resisted the temptation to proclaim an 'official' answer at that point.

So this episode ended with an acknowledgement of the children having different conceptions. To have tried to smooth these over might have resulted in the rest of the group simply playing lip-service to Joseph's thinking and starting on the slippery road of feeling that what is 'correct' in mathematics need not quite make sense.

What other things are commonly done, supposedly to simplify things for children, which in fact prove to be counterproductive?

Perhaps if we need to provide an 'end of a session' focus, we could make use of a forward-looking comment such as 'How might we carry on next time?' 'We'll have to think again about these different answers then', etc.

A FINAL POINT

This chapter might give the impression that I am always satisfied with the decisions I have made and the actions I have taken in sessions. That is far from the case. Often when I analyse an activity afterwards, particularly if I listen to a recording of it, I become aware of a number of things which I wish I had tackled differently.

I commented in chapter 2 that I had included the 'Plates of biscuits' case-study (chapter 7) as an example of a session which left me with worries. I have mentioned some of my qualms about it in the discussions in chapter 9 (p. 99) and chapter 10 (p. 115) but giving a list here of some of the questions I am left with might be of interest as they centre on some under-lying concerns:

- Was there any way in which I could have involved the children in conjecturing and testing their conjectures, without leading them so much?
- The children did not respond when I asked them what was special about the numbers Ilona had used (p. 64). Did they feel they had already

expressed what was salient to them and were puzzled by my question?
- Was Ilona left behind at some points? How could this have been avoided?
- Having marked Jemma's answers on his number ladder, Sam noted that there were only two numbers between the first two but three between the rest (p. 72). How could I have avoided telling the children to forget about the two at the bottom? That smacked of their having to do something without any particular reason.

All of these questions can themselves lead to other questions, wider in scope. For example, out of the second one can grow, 'How can we become more sensitive in discerning what it is inappropriate to ask?' Such wider questions are, of course, not just relevant to the activity from which they grew initially, but to all later activities. Indeed, what is perhaps the most important feature of feeling uneasy about a session is the constructive help this can give in enabling one to focus on points for future attention. Not that there are likely to be easily obtained, cut and dried answers to many of the questions raised, but striving to tease out and grapple with some of the complexity will perhaps make us more alert to possibilities.

IN CONCLUSION: WHY?

To write a summary as a form of 'conclusion' would run the risk of leaving the reader with a dangerously oversimplified and closed picture of the complex situations already discussed. Moreover, in the sense that this book aims to influence readers' own thinking it has no 'end'.

There is, however, one particular theme which I think could benefit from further crystallisation at this stage: so far, many of the reasons for wanting young children to work in an active way at mathematics have been merely implicit in what has been written. The issue can be stated more fully here, drawing together threads from different parts of the book.

In the preface to this book there is a quotation from the Department of Education and Science's publication *Mathematics from 5 to 16* (1985). The document claims that we should aim 'to show mathematics as a process, as a creative activity in which pupils can be fully involved, and not as an imposed body of knowledge, immune to any change or development' (p. 4). This provides an immediate reason for encouraging young children to participate in steering their own mathematical activities: it is recommended that we should teach mathematics like this to all children.

Perhaps, however, we can probe more deeply? Three further reasons emerge from the following points:

- If the emphasis is on the teacher taking the lead all the time, children's abilities to manage set questions and to obtain correct answers may mask an actual lack of understanding, becoming the basis of problems at a later stage.
- If children cannot complete a teacher-designed task, not only have they not carried out the task, they have also not lived up to the teacher's hope for success. If children cannot successfully complete their *own* ideas at present, this does not seem to carry with it the same sense of failure.
- A teacher can never be certain of the appropriateness of a prescribed task to the children concerned or of their understanding of it. Children's own questions and ideas will be meaningful and relevant to them.

It might be constructive to begin to compare some features of mathematics itself with some points about young children's capabilities gleaned from the case-studies and discussions of other examples in this book. It is important to note that when referring to mathematics below, I have in mind the wide view of the subject implicit in mathematics as an activity. To distinguish this from any narrower views the word mathematics will be set in italic.

MATHEMATICS	*YOUNG CHILDREN*
The making of conjectures; structuring; deciding on rules, etc. is essential to *mathematics*.	Young children engage naturally in these processes.
Engaging in *mathematics* involves one in developing mathematical ideas; questioning; exploring; initiating ideas, methods and symbols oneself; and attempting to control apparently chaotic or muddled data.	Young children are naturally eager and curious and are able to invent and sustain activities themselves.
A major concern in *mathematics* is to be consistent.	Young children are intrigued by inconsistencies and attempt to sort them out.
Mathematics is not bounded. It is not confined to the material world.	Young children can go beyond the immediate and familiar, showing imagination and an ability to make their own generalisations from particulars.
Mathematics is a challenging intellectual activity.	Young children often take tasks upon themselves which we would be wary of setting, then show determination in tackling them.
What is correct in *mathematics* depends on the context. Different decisions and assumptions can lead to different results.	Young children can appreciate that more than one answer can be right at once. Questions can be ambiguous and need interpretation.
Mathematics is not rigidly compartmentalised.	Young children can become involved in a wide range of skills and ideas within the same short space of time. They can forge a rich variety of connections and view items from different angles.
Mathematics is not a mindless activity. For example, there are sensible reasons for the introduction of notations and terminology.	Young children can work with a purpose. For example, they are capable of seeing a need for new terms and symbols and for modifying usage of familiar ones.

In *mathematics* one can push forward one's own thinking. One does not have to keep to set methods etc.	When not constrained by continually having to work out and provide 'what the teacher wants' within a closed context, young children are often willing to have a go, make suggestions, etc.

This is only a beginning. What else could be added?

It is clear that there is a match across each pair of entries in the two columns above. Characteristics of *mathematics* are evident in young children's activities. If we teach mathematics only in the narrow senses of passing it on passively as a body of knowledge, or formally as a symbol-system, we are doing a disservice both to the nature of this human activity and to young children's natural capabilities and considerable powers.

APPENDIX

When the children carried out the mathematical activities described in this book, the National Curriculum had not been published. Now that it has been, it might be of interest to consider the children's work in the light of the attainment targets specified in the statutory orders for mathematics (see Department of Education and Science, *Mathematics in the National Curriculum*, 1989). In doing this, however, we must remember that 7 is the age at which children will first be formally assessed, so we would not necessarily expect any of the attainment targets to be appropriate to 4 and 5 year olds. Providing we keep reminding ourselves of that fact, however, we can still ask the question: are there any connections between what the children have shown themselves able to do and the National Curriculum?

I shall explore this question in relation to the first case-study in part II, the 'Circle arrangements' activity. In analysing this episode in terms of the attainment targets I can see evidence of children being involved in

Counting, reading and writing numbers

Examples:

Sam and Matthew count up to eighty-one circles and discuss how to write '81'; Jemma counts nine circles in the rectangles; Ilona makes sense of what Jemma has written: 'There are "p" sets of 2 dots'. Sam realises that the 'p' should have been the other way round and writes it as '9'.

This links with:

AT2: Number, Level 1: Count, read, write and order numbers to at least 10.
AT2: Number, Level 2: Read, write and order numbers to at least 100.

Recognising that a number of objects can be arranged in different ways

Example:

All the children make different arrangements of the number of circles they have chosen to colour.

This links with:
AT2: Number, Level 1: Understand the conservation of number.

Informal subtraction

Examples:
When Jemma shades in six circles instead of four, Ilona tells her to 'Cross two out.' Matthew works out that he is colouring in more spots than Sam is, commenting, 'I've got more than you: six, seven, eight.'

This links with:
AT3: Number, Level 1: Add or subtract, using objects where numbers involved are not greater than 10.
AT3: Number, Level 2: Know and use addition and subtraction facts up to 10. Compare two numbers to find the difference.

Patterning

Example:
Ilona makes a pattern when shading in the sets of six spots on her sheet.

This links with:
AT5: Algebra, Level 1: Copy, continue and devise repeating patterns.

Setting tasks, comparing, describing and checking

Examples:
All the children set themselves tasks, talk about their work and write about some aspect of it. Matthew describes his eight circles problem to Sam. Both boys check their sheets against each other's and produce two more examples.

This links with:
AT1&9: Using and Applying Mathematics, Level 1: Talk about own work and ask questions.
AT1&9: Using and Applying Mathematics, Level 2: Describe work, record findings and check results.

Using terms for shapes

Example:
The children talk of 'circles' at the beginning of the episode and there is a brief discussion about the use of the words 'square', 'hexagon' and 'rectangle'.

This links with:

AT10: Shape and Space, Level 2: Recognise squares, rectangles, circles, triangles, hexagons, pentagons, cubes, cuboids, cylinders and spheres and describe them.

Putting the same shape in different positions

Example:

Sam puts his pattern of five circles in different positions and explains the differences.

This links with:

AT11: Shape and Space, Level 2: Recognise different types of movement: straight movement, turning movement and flip.

More examples?

You might like to analyse some of the other case-studies . . . or your own . . . in terms of the National Curriculum.

NOTES

1 SOME QUESTIONS

1 This example has been taken from Bird (1983), p. 55. For further details of the activity see Bird (1981).

9 THE MATHEMATICS

1 This example is taken from Bird (1983), p. 34.
2 For further details see, for example, Kneebone (1963).
3 For an account of this activity see Bird (1986), chapter 2.
4 I am grateful to Professor H. B. Griffiths for his discussion of this example with me.
5 I have, however, come across some examples where young infants *do* seem to have a feeling for the fact that a situation has been exhausted so it would be impossible to do more. For example, on one occasion a group of children were making 'houses' using a square and triangle of gummed paper for each one. At one point, they kept trying to make different houses: 'different' in terms of the colours used for the square and the triangle. As there were only yellow and green squares available and yellow and blue triangles, there were just four combinations. After the children had made those four houses, I tried not to convey that I realised they had accounted for the possibilities and invited them to make another house. After a little while, Clive (4.11) became quite indignant and asserted 'We can't do them different.' What he then said and pointed to suggested that he had perceived that the yellow squares had been used with both the yellow and blue triangles and that the green squares had been used with both the yellow and blue triangles. He seemed thoroughly convinced that it would be impossible to make any more houses without using other colours.

This example is even more remarkable when we reflect on the fact that some post 'A' level students do not readily make a distinction between situations of the 'I've-been-looking-for-a-long-time-and-I-can't-find-any-more' sort and situations in which one can say that it would be impossible to find any more. Perhaps we need to be more alert to the fact that children as young as 4 and 5 can be aware of 'impossibility' in the sense discussed above, and encourage the development of their insights?

6 A fuller description is given in Bird (1980). It needs to be borne in mind that this is a write-up-after-the-event, not an account of my explorations-as-they-were-happening. Hence there is little indication of all the trial and error initially involved, nor of the many modifications I had to make to my ideas as I proceeded.

11 THE TEACHER'S ROLE

1 Brenda Briggs suggested this very helpful phrase.

2 I am very grateful to the following: the class teacher, Betty Jackson; the head-teacher, Eira Gill; Brenda Briggs from the University of Southampton; my colleagues at West Sussex Institute of Higher Education, in particular Afzal Ahmed; numerous teachers on in-service courses; teacher-fellows and research-ers, in particular Jayne Ross; numerous B.Ed. students at the Institute.

3 For example, see Russell (1919).

4 Booklets containing starting-points suitable for young infants include Hatch (1984) and Bird (1987).

5 See Bird (1983) and Bird (1986).

6 I first became aware of the distinctions discussed here when reading Skemp (1971).

7 See, for example, the research carried out by (1) M. R. Lepper; and (2) R. Anderson, S. T. Manoogia and J. S. Reznick; as discussed in Donaldson (1984), pp. 115–17.

BIBLIOGRAPHY

Some of the following texts have been included because references have already been made to them. The others have been listed because they played a part in the development of the ideas expressed in this book. The ten texts marked with an asterisk were of particular significance to my thinking.

Armstrong, M. (1980) *Closely observed children – the diary of a primary classroom*, Oxford: Oxford University Press.

Association of Teachers of Mathematics (1967) *Notes on mathematics in primary schools*, Cambridge: Cambridge University Press.

Association of Teachers of Mathematics (1977) *Notes on mathematics for children*, Cambridge: Cambridge University Press.

Barnes, D. (1975) *From communication to curriculum*, Harmondsworth: Penguin.

Barnes, D., Britton, J., and Torbe, M. (1986) *Language, the learner and the school*, Harmondsworth: Penguin (third edition).

Bell, A. W., Shiu, C. M., and Horton, B. (1981) *Evaluating attainment in process aspects of mathematics*, Shell Centre for Mathematical Education: University of Nottingham.

Bennett, N., Desforges, C., Cockburn, A., and Wilkinson, R. (1984) *The quality of pupil learning experiences*, Lawrence Erlbaum Associates.

Bernstein, B. (1983) *Beyond objectivism and relativism*, Oxford: Basil Blackwell.

Bird, M. H. (1980) 'A new look at functions in modular arithmetic', *The Mathematical Gazette* 64(428).

Bird, M. H. (1981) 'An odd number of factors', *Mathematics Teaching* 95.

Bird, M. H. (1983) *Generating mathematical activity in the classroom*, West Sussex Institute of Higher Education (reprinted by The Mathematical Association).

Bird, M. H. (1986) *Mathematics with seven and eight year olds*, Leicester: The Mathematical Association.

Bird, M. H. (1987) *Openings: some ideas which have been used with four and five year olds to stimulate mathematical activity*, West Sussex Institute of Higher Education.

Bloor, D. (1983) 'Mathematics: an anthropological phenomenon', *Wittgenstein: a social theory of knowledge*, London: The Macmillan Press, Chapter 5.

Britton, J. (1970) *Language and learning*, Harmondsworth: Penguin.

Bruner, J.S.* (1966) *Toward a theory of instruction*, Cambridge, Mass.: Harvard University Press.

Burgess, R. G. (ed.) (1985) *Strategies of educational research*, London: The Falmer Press.

Byers, V. and Erlwanger, S. (1984) 'Content and form in mathematics', *Educational Studies in Mathematics* 15(3).

Carr, W. and Kemmis, S.* (1986) *Becoming critical*, London: The Falmer Press.

Cockcroft, W. H. (1982) *Report of the Committee of Inquiry into the teaching of mathematics in schools: mathematics counts*, London: HMSO.

Cohen, L. and Manion, L. (1984) *Research methods in education*, London: Croom Helm (second edition).

Courant, R. and Robbins, H. (1978) *What is mathematics?* Oxford: Oxford University Press (paperback edition).

Davis, P. J. and Hersh, R.* (1981) *The mathematical experience*, Harmondsworth: Penguin.

Davis, R., Golby, M., Kernig, W., and Tamburrini, J. (1986) 'The infant school: past, present and future', *Bedford Way Papers* (27) Institute of Education, University of London.

Desforges, C. and Cockburn, A. (1987) *Understanding the mathematics teacher: A study of practice in First Schools*, London: The Falmer Press.

Department of Education and Science (1985) *Mathematics from 5 to 16*, London: HMSO.

Department of Education and Science (1989) *Mathematics in the National Curriculum*, London: HMSO.

Dickson, L., Brown, M., and Gibson, O. (1984) *Children learning mathematics: A teacher's guide to recent research*, London: Holt, Rinehart & Winston for the Schools Council.

Dienes, Z. P. (1964) *The power of mathematics*, London: Hutchinson Educational.

Donaldson, M.* (1984) *Children's minds*, London: Flamingo (second edition).

Donaldson, M., Grieve, R., and Pratt, C. (eds) (1983) *Early childhood development and education: readings in psychology*, Oxford: Basil Blackwell.

Dowling, M. and Dauncey, E. (1984) *Teaching three to nine year olds*, London: Ward Lock Educational Ltd.

Edwards, A. D. and Furlong, V. J. (1978) *The language of teaching: meaning in classroom interaction*, London: Heinemann.

Foster, J. (1972) *Discovery learning in the primary school*, London: Routledge & Kegan Paul.

Freudenthal, H. (1973) *Mathematics as an educational task*, Dordrecht, Holland: D. Reidel.

Freudenthal, H.* (1983) *Didactical phenomenology of mathematical structures*, Dordrecht, Holland: D. Reidel.

Freudenthal, H. (1987) *Mathematics observed*, London: Weidenfeld & Nicholson.

Galton, M., Simon, B., and Croll, P. (1980) *Inside the primary classroom*, London: Routledge & Kegan Paul.

Gattegno, C. (1963) *For the teaching of mathematics* (Volumes 1, 2, and 3), Reading: Educational Explorers Ltd.

Gelman, R. and Gallistel, C. R. (1978) *The child's understanding of number*, Cambridge, Mass.: Harvard University Press.

Getzels, J. W. and Jackson, P. W. (1962) *Creativity and intelligence*, London: Wiley.

Ghieslin, B. (ed.) (1985) *The creative process – a symposium*, Berkeley, CA: University of California Press.

Goutard, M. (1964) *Mathematics and children*, Reading: Educational Explorers Ltd.

Griffiths, H. B. (1983) 'Simplification and complexity in mathematics education', *Educational Studies in Mathematics* 14(3).

Groen, G. and Resnick, L. B. (1977) 'Can pre-school children invent addition algorithms?' *Journal of Educational Psychology* 69(6).

Habermas, J. (1974) *Theory and practice*, London: Heinemann.

Hadamard, J. (1945) *The psychology of invention in the mathematical field*, New York: Dover.

Hammersley, M. (ed.) (1986) *Case studies in classroom research*, Milton Keynes: The Open University.

Hann, G. H. (1972) 'What is mathematics?', *Mathematics Teaching* (60).

Hann, G. H. (1977) 'A critique of Piaget's work on the development of mathematical and logical thinking', unpublished Ph.D thesis, University of London.

Hatch, G. (1984) *Bounce to it! A collection of investigations and problems for infants*, Manchester: Manchester Polytechnic.

Hawkins, D. (1974) *The informed vision: essays on learning and human nature*, New York: Agathon Press.

Hawkins, D.* (1985) 'The edge of Platonism', *For the learning of mathematics* 5(2).

Haylock, D. W. (1987) 'A framework for assessing mathematical creativity in school-children' *Educational Studies in Mathematics* 18(1).

Holt, J.* (1984) *How children fail*, Harmondsworth: Penguin (revised edition).

Hopkins, D. (1985) *A teacher's guide to classroom research*, Oxford: Oxford University Press.

Hughes, M. (1981) 'Can pre-school children add and subtract?' *Educational Psychology* 1(3).

Hughes, M. (1983) 'Teaching arithmetic to pre-school children', *Educational Review* 35(2).

Hughes, M. (1986) *Children and number: difficulties in learning mathematics*, Oxford: Basil Blackwell.

King, R. (1978) *All things bright and beautiful: a sociological study of infants' classrooms*, London: Wiley.

Kitcher, P. (1984) *The nature of mathematical knowledge*, Oxford: Oxford University Press.

Klenk, V. H. (1976) *Wittgenstein's philosophy of mathematics*, The Hague: Martinus Nijhoff.

Kneebone, G. T. (1963) *Mathematical logic and the foundations of mathematics*, London: D. Van Nostrand.

Kneller, G. F. (1966) *The art and science of creativity*, London: Holt, Rinehart and Winston.

Korner, S. (1968) *The philosophy of mathematics*, London: Hutchinson University Library.

Krutetskii, V. A. (1976) *The psychology of mathematical abilities in schoolchildren*, Chicago: University of Chicago Press.

Kuhn, T. S. (1970) 'The structure of scientific revolutions', *International Encyclopaedia of Unified Science* 2(2) The University of Chicago Press.

Lakatos, I.* (1976) *Proofs and refutations: the logic of mathematical discovery*, Cambridge: Cambridge University Press.

Low Attainers in Mathematics Project (1987) *Better mathematics: a curriculum development study*, London: HMSO.

Merleau-Ponty, M. (1962) *Phenomenology of perception*. London: Routledge & Kegan Paul.

Opie, I. and Opie, P. (1984) *Children's games in street and playground*, Oxford: Oxford University Press.

Papert, S. (1980) *Mindstorms*, Brighton: The Harvester Press.

Poincaré, H. (1970) 'Mathematical creation', in P. E. Vernon (ed.) *Creativity*, Harmondsworth: Penguin.

Polanyi, M. (1976) *Personal knowledge*, London: Routledge & Kegan Paul.

Pollard, A. (ed.) (1987) *Children and their primary schools*, London: The Falmer Press.

Pollard, A. (1988) 'Reflective teaching: the sociological contribution', in P. Woods (ed.) *Sociology and teaching*, London: Croom Helm.

Pollard, A. and Tarn, S. (1987) *Reflective teaching in the primary school*, London: Cassell.

Rowland, S. (1984) *The enquiring classroom: An introduction to children's learning*, London: The Falmer Press.

Russell, B. (1919) *Introduction to mathematical philosophy*, London: George Allen & Unwin.

Schutz, A.* (1972) *The phenomenology of the social world*, London: Heinemann.

Schutz, A. (1973) *Collected papers I: The problem of social reality*, The Hague: Martinus Nijhoff.

Shipman, M. (ed.) (1985) *Educational research: principles, policies and practices*, London: The Falmer Press.

Shipman, M. (1985) *The management of learning in the classroom*, London: Hodder & Stoughton.

Shuard, H. (1986) *Primary mathematics today and tomorrow*, London: Longman for the School Curriculum Development Committee.

Simons, H. (ed.) (1980) *Towards a science of the singular*, University of East Anglia: Centre for Applied Research in Education, Occasional publication number 10.

Skemp, R. R. (1971) *The psychology of learning mathematics*, Harmondsworth: Penguin.

Tammadge, A. (1979) 'Creativity', *The mathematical gazette* 63(425).

Tizard, B. and Hughes, M.* (1984) *Young children learning: talking and thinking at home and at school*, London: Fontana.

Tough, J. (1976) 'Listening to children talking', from the *Schools Council Communication skills in early childhood project*, London: Ward Lock Educational.

Underwood, V. (1966) 'Children's mathematical activity', from *The development of mathematical activity in children*, Association of Teachers of Mathematics.

Van Den Brink, F. J. (1984) 'Acoustic counting and quantity counting', *For the Learning of Mathematics* 4.

Van Den Brink, F. J. (1984) 'Numbers in contextual frameworks', *Educational Studies in Mathematics* 15(3).

Vygotsky, L. S. (1962) *Thought and language*, Cambridge, Mass.: M.I.T. Press.

Waddington, C. H. (1977) *Tools for thought*, London: Paladin.

Walkerdine, V. (1981) *Practice of reason, part 1: reading the signs of mathematics*, London: Bedford Way Publications.

Westcott, A. M. (1978) *Creative teaching of mathematics in the elementary school*, Boston: Allyn and Bacon.

White, J. P. (1975) 'Creativity and education: a philosophical analysis', in R. F. Dearden, P. H. Hirst, and R. S. Peters (eds) *A critique of current educational aims*, London: Routledge & Kegan Paul.

Wittgenstein, L. (1939) *Wittgenstein's lectures on the foundations of mathematics, Cambridge 1939*, Hassocks: Harvester Press 1976.

Yardley, A. (1973) *Young children thinking*, London: Evans Brothers.

Yates, J. (1978) *Four mathematical classrooms: an enquiry into teaching method*, University of Southampton.

INDEX

References are made to items within parts I and III. Items within part II have not been indexed since salient features of the case-studies are drawn out and analysed in part III and cross-referenced at that point.

CAN INVESTIGATIVE MATHS SURVIVE WITH THE NATIONAL CURRICULUM?

HOW CAN TEACHERS ENCOURAGE YOUNG CHILDREN'S ACTIVE MATHEMATICAL THINKING?

This book shows how children as young as four and five of all abilities can be encouraged to carry out their own mathematical explorations whilst at the same time covering the content of a prescribed curriculum. It includes a selection of case studies from the author's own work with young children and a wide range of examples of children's work. Throughout, readers are encouraged to apply and amend the ideas it contains to suit their own particular circumstances.

Marion H. Bird is Senior Lecturer in mathematics education at the West Sussex Institute of Higher Education.

Education

Cover design: Alan Forster
Cover photograph: © Sally and Richard Greenhill

ROUTLEDGE

11 New Fetter Lane
London EC4P 4EE

29 West 35th Street
New York NY 10001

ISBN 0-415-05951-8

9 780415 059510